The Red and the White

Also from
Temple of Justice Books

Alchemy in Middle-earth:
The Significance of J.R.R. Tolkien's
The Lord of the Rings

Mahmoud Shelton

The Red and the White

Perspectives on America
and the Primordial Tradition

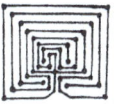

Temple of Justice Books

Copyright © 2019 D.M. Shelton

All rights reserved. This book or any portion thereof may not be reproduced or used in any manner whatsoever without the express written permission of the publisher.

Temple of Justice Books
templeofjustice@icloud.com

Printed in the United States of America

ISBN 978-0-9741468-1-2

Contents

1	White Indians?	7
2	New Worlds	17
3	Moon Watchers	27
4	People of the Mounds	37
5	Fixing the Earth	47
6	Stones of Exile	57
7	Between East and West	69
8	Treasures of Red and White	79
9	The Western Phoenix	89

"And give unto me a sincere report in the last generations."

The Prophet Abraham
Qur'an XXVI, 84

1

White Indians?

By the end of the 20th century, America seemed to have no serious rival in the world, and be self-satisfied in its success. For the United States, America's history begins in 1492 with the opening of the lands of the Western Hemisphere to European conquest. Before this date, a Latin phrase had long warned all who looked west beyond the Pillars of Hercules at the limit of Europe: "Ne Plus Ultra," meaning "no further." Rejecting this warning, Spain was the first to profit in the New World, and Charles V soon adopted the motto "Plus Ultra" in his ambitions.[1] Challenging Spain was its principal rival, Britain; in service to HM Elizabeth I, the magus Dr. John Dee became the architect of what he himself dubbed the "British Empire." According to Dr. Dee, the British claim to America enjoyed precedence over the Spanish since it was founded upon the legendary medieval voyage of Prince Madoc of Wales. Dee mentioned in the context of this claim that the New World was none other than "the ancient Atlantis, no longer – nowe named America,"[2] and so alluded to a prehistory of significant depth.

---

[1] While this motto may be overlooked, the Imperial design bearing these words – with its sinusoidal ribbon in front of two pillars - bears an unmistakable similarity to the dollar sign, that is, the sign of American supremacy.

[2] Quoted in Robert W. Barone, "Madoc and John Dee: Welsh Myth and Elizabethan Imperialism," *Elizabethan Review*.

A magus of the reign of HM Elizabeth II, the late John Michell, commented on the conquest of America in his seminal work *The New View Over Atlantis*, first published in 1969:

> The European colonists in North America were, perhaps, the first to exterminate the native inhabitants without learning the secrets of their geomancy, of the seasons proper for invoking the fertilizing influences and of the sacred spots appropriate for that purpose...The catastrophic results of the North Americans' failure to inherit the geomantic lore of their predecessors is now becoming apparent in the endemic restlessness and unease of the present inhabitants and in the approach of sterility to both land and livestock through the application of naïve agricultural theories, together with the disregard on the part of politicians, generals and industrialists for the living, and therefore vulnerable, nature of the country they inhabit.[3]

Now in the early years of the 21st century, it is indeed the chronic disregard for nature that presents America with perhaps its greatest challenges in confronting a changing climate. This is, moreover, a direct consequence of the European conquest: recent research establishes a clear link between the massacre of American Indians and the first historic effect of humanity upon greenhouse gases;[4] and it goes without saying that the plundering of the New World

---

[3] Pages 199-200.

[4] Koch, et al., "Earth System Impacts of the European Arrival and Great Dying in the Americas After 1492," *Quaternary Science Reviews*, volume 2017, 1 March 2019, pages 13-36.

made the Industrial Revolution possible, the effects of which are only now becoming obvious. From the American Indian perspective, such behavior is not altogether surprising:

> It was well within the range of human beings to become greedy in the face of abundance and fall into hubris in light of the independence that it permitted, rather than being careful of the interdependence that underlay this autonomy. Unrestrained, humans broke the law, violated the pure and reliable order of the world, polluting it, bringing floods, starvation, and death...[5]

Throughout 2016, a remarkable standoff took place on the Standing Rock Reservation in North Dakota, in which the largest gathering of American Indians in a century protested the imposition of a gas pipeline that would endanger water and desecrate the landscape; but in 2017, a newly inaugurated President Trump insisted on the pipeline's completion. The failure of the protest was rather more essentially a final failure of the American government to show higher regard for the natural order than for its corporate interests, and to offer reconciliation with those who for so long faced de facto genocide.[6]

At Standing Rock, the tribes insisted that the protest was above all an expression of their identity, an identity separate from that of white America, and indeed opposed to predominantly white government and corporations. This divide between "red" and white America, seemingly so permanent, was strangely and wishfully bridged back at its

---

[5] Thomas Buckley, *Standing Ground: Yurok Indian Spirituality, 1850-1990*, Berkeley: University of California Press, 2002, page 214.

[6] This failure is all the more striking when it is recalled that the only tribe to have adopted a president – Calvin Coolidge - was the very tribe that Trump refused to defend, the Standing Rock Sioux.

beginnings, since the claim of Prince Madoc's landing gave rise to a legend of Welsh, and therefore white, Indians. Rumors of their survival were commonplace, but the discovery of these "White Indians" remained elusive. Despite the continued search for such a tribe being included in the mandate from President Jefferson for Lewis and Clark's expedition, the hope for its discovery retreated ever westward, until its ghostly existence was eclipsed by a Manifest Destiny unconcerned with the fate of Indians.[7]

Nevertheless, this legend had in fact eclipsed in the young American consciousness authentic Indian lore. According to James Mooney in his *Myths of the Cherokee* of 1902, "there is a dim but persistent tradition of a strange white race preceding the Cherokee, some of the stories even going so far as to locate their former settlements and to identify them as the authors of the ancient works found in the country;" and indeed, it was none other than these same "ancient works" of unmortared stone that had provided ample proof of the Welsh Indians for those who sought traces of their movements. Alternatively called the "Moon-eyed People" or "White People" – although these designations are much the same, since white is the color of the moon - Mooney relates from several sources that this community "agreed to remove if they were allowed to depart in peace," and "finally went west, 'long before the whites came.'"[8]

Mooney also mentions that others sought to explain the dominant characteristic of these people as the result of albinism, or of their preference for circular houses in the earth. There is a more important indication, however, in the description of their apparent preference for peace. Cherokee

---

[7] In connection with the persistence of Madoc, it is at least curious that the fiercest resistance to the new American forces of conquest in the furthest west belonged to a people called Modoc. For some reason this name also appears at an Indian site near the Mississippi River that is unconnected to the California tribe that was relocated to Oklahoma.

[8] Pages 22-3.

society was traditionally divided into two groups, the red and the white.[9] The former designated those partaking in the duties of war, who in turn were dependent upon the latter to be purified upon the fulfillment of their duties. This "white" group was priestly and indeed hereditary and responsible for healing and preserving peace.[10] In other words, this society exemplified the proper relationship between the royal and sacerdotal castes, as was originally known in traditional India with its Brahmin and Kshatriya. However, these distinctions had apparently been lost so long ago that modern Cherokee, according to Mooney, know so little about this sacerdotal caste "that their very identity is now a matter of dispute, a few holding that they were an ancient people who preceded the Cherokee and built the mounds." Remarkably, Mooney traces the end of this sacerdotal caste to a violent revolt against them.[11]

These sacerdotal and warrior roles have a symbolic relationship with the night and day. The night may be understood to correspond to the sacerdotal, since the night is the time of quiet and contemplation, and pertains to the mysteries of the unseen. The day, of course, is the proper time for action in the world. However, even though it has been observed that the traditional sacerdotal caste of the Cherokee was associated with the night, the reason for this has escaped the author of the following comment: "Night of course, is associated with magic and danger, with darkness and the moon, and with death and chaos, whereas daytime is related to religious propitiation..."[12] Amidst such confusion,

---

[9] This structure was likewise known among the Creek.

[10] The use of white as a sacerdotal emblem in fact appears throughout Indian America, the Iroquois White Tree of Peace and White Buffalo Woman of the Plains Indians being two additional examples.

[11] Ibid., page 392.

[12] Raymond D. Fogelson, "Who were the Aní-Kutání? An Excursus into Cherokee Historical Thought," *Ethnohistory*, volume 31, number 4, Autumn 1984, page 259.

even though the moon is here specifically mentioned, the echo between the fate of this caste and that of the Moon-eyed People has apparently gone unnoticed.

The Cherokee memory of an ancient white people is by no means an isolated tradition. Remarkably similar memories may be found in the furthest west along the Pacific coast. The following account, for example, concerns the arrival of the Chetko to the mouth of the river bearing their name:

> They found two tribes in possession, one a warlike race, resembling themselves; these they soon conquered and exterminated. The other was a diminutive people, of an exceedingly mild disposition, and white. These called themselves, or were called by the newcomers, "Wogies." They were skillful in the manufacture of baskets, robes, and canoes, and had many methods of taking game and fish unknown to the invaders. Refusing to fight, the Wogies were made slaves of...the more warlike race...One night, however...the Wogies packed up and fled, and were never more seen.[13]

We are especially indebted to the even more remarkable account of Lucy Thompson, who related a wealth of knowledge belonging to the Yurok tribe about these "ancient white people" that is astonishing when compared to the dim recollections of the Cherokee:

> When the Indians first made their appearance on the Klamath River it was

---

[13] This 1873 account was cited by Stephen Powers in his important 1877 work to be considered below (*Tribes of California*, Berkeley: University of California Press, 1976, page 69).

White Indians?

already inhabited by a white race of people known among us as the Wa-gas. These white people were found to inhabit the whole continent, and were a highly moral and civilized race. They heartily welcomed the Indians to their country and taught us all of their arts and sciences...After a time there were inter-marriages between the two races...For a vast period of time the two races dwelt together in peace...as the white people ruled with beacon light of kindness, and our people still worship the hallowed places where once they trod...After we had lived with these ancient people so long, they suddenly called their hosts together and mysteriously disappeared for a distant land, we know not where...On leaving they went toward the North from whence we came...In their farewell journey across this land they left landmarks of stone monuments, on the tops of high mountains and places commanding a view of the surrounding country. These land-marks we have kept in repair, down through the ages in loving remembrance...[14]

Given the known migrations during various periods of tribes such as the Cherokee, the assertion of anteriority for the white people may only be relative, especially since the Chetko, for example, had also found people like themselves living with the "Wogies." Obviously the manner of interacting with these white people has varied. What must be

---

[14] *To the American Indian: Reminiscences of a Yurok Woman*, 1916, pages 64-5. Thompson also relates that in Yurok myth the first creature on earth was the white deer, followed by the red eagle, indicating the primacy of spiritual authority.

insisted upon, however, is the consistent report of their character and works drawn from regions very far removed. The similarities are distinctive. For example, it is accepted that "religious language in the Southeast frequently has a sacerdotal quality attributable to alien speech;"[15] and in California, the Yurok "spoke prayers and sang songs just as the Wo'gey had done,"[16] and who moreover "use a special, ritual register of Yurok, wo-gey speech, in which they spoke from a wo-gey perspective.[17] Among the Cherokee, this language is so unusual that the very name of the sacerdotal caste – the Aní-Kutánî or "People of Kutánî" – has an unknown etymology. The hereditary character of this caste may even be echoed by the focus of the Yurok elite: "Aristocratic Indians sought to emulate the Wo'gey in all things."[18]

Concerning the works attributed to the ancient white people, many remain to this day, but these are often overlooked.[19] President Jackson – Trump's favorite predecessor – had cited "the monuments and fortresses of an unknown people, spread over the extensive regions of the West" as justification for his notorious policies, since the new Americans claimed to simply be succeeding the Indians as conquerors.[20] Yet the identity of this "unknown people" has

---

[15] Fogelson, op. cit., page 255-6.
[16] Richard Keeling, *Cry for Luck: Sacred Song and Speech Among the Yurok, Hupa, and Karok Indians of Northwestern California*, Berkeley: University of California Press, 1992, page 20.
[17] Buckley, op. cit., page 215.
[18] Keeling, page 20.
[19] Resisting this trend, the work of the academic Harry Holstein in lands associated with the Cherokee and Creek deserves to be mentioned. For him, the stone monuments are Pan-American proofs of Indian religion, and so he works to preserve them.
[20] First Annual Message to Congress, 8 December 1830. Although the hilltop constructions attributed to the ancient white people have routinely been identified as "stone forts," even cursory examination

left its traces not only upon the landscape but also in American Indian memory, as we have seen; and the Yurok at least confronted the tragic irony that the American people of European origin had white skin, and so were likewise called Wo'gey:

> When the present race of the white people made their first appearance upon the American continent, we believed it was the Wa-gas returning and a hearty welcome was extended to them and there was great rejoicing among our tribes. But soon the sad mistake was discovered to our sorrow...We no longer termed them as Wa-gas, but as Ken-e-yahs, which means foreigners, who had no right to the land and could never appreciate our kindness, for they were a very different people from the Wa-gas. They had corrupt morals that brought dissolution upon our people and wrought the horrors of untold havoc.[21]

So the new Americans were recognized as an unmistakable parody of an ancient presence, and it is only in serving to make this parody recognizable that the uncertain racial identity of the ancient people has any relevance for us here. Nevertheless, the understanding of this parody may very well open a new view on traditional America.

---

suggests that their function was not military; nevertheless, they may have appropriately constituted a kind of sacerdotal "defense."
[21] Thompson, page 66.

Che-na-wah Weitch-ah-wah of the Yurok
Mrs. Lucy Thompson

2

New Worlds

Dr. Dee's assertion that the newly opened world of America was none other than ancient Atlantis seems rather straightforward; after all, what land would be found west of the Pillars of Hercules if not the one described by Plato? However, the very existence of America seems to contradict Plato's account of the disappearance of Atlantis. For his part, John Michell names Atlantis in the very title of his seminal work, but America is not its primary focus, since his attention is concerned above all with the geomancy mysteriously encoded in the ancient landmarks – megalithic and otherwise – of his native Britain. As his later writings indicate, Michell would become indebted to the work of René Guénon, who he calls "the great esoteric scholar," in particular concerning matters pertaining to the Grail and its link to the "Primordial Tradition."[1] Perhaps if he had recourse to Guénon's works when he wrote *The View Over Atlantis*, Michell would have had a great deal more to say on the subject.

Precise references to Atlantis are in fact sprinkled throughout the oeuvre of René Guénon. Part of his mission was to describe the true nature of the modern world, and in order to do so Guénon made recourse to the Hindu doctrine of cosmic cycles, the most sophisticated model for understanding the rhythms of time. Nevertheless, he would use terms more familiar to the Western mentality whenever

---

[1] John Michell and Christine Rhone, *Twelve-Tribe Nations and the Science of Enchanting the Landscape*, London: Thames and Hudson Ltd., 1991, especially pages 9 and 72.

suitable, and so he employed the term "Hyperborean" to refer to the original formulation of the Primordial Tradition; he used "Atlantis" to refer to a subsequent development of that tradition, with distinct symbolic characteristics.[2] Most essentially, the Hyperborean tradition was characterized by a northern orientation, and so emphasizes a polar dimension, whereas the Atlantean orientation was western, as we have already noted. According to Guénon, what has complicated matters is the persistence of names once belonging to the Hyperborean tradition into the Atlantean period, or indeed into much more recent times. Such is the example of the "primeval Syria," perhaps a better name for Hyperborea itself, and of Tula, a primary designation for a spiritual center.[3] Much clearer was the reason for the destruction of Atlantis: the revolt of its warrior caste against the sacerdotal, a revolt with echoes throughout the ages.

René Guénon further clarifies matters by identifying the Biblical Deluge, at least in its most literal formulation, with the cataclysm of Atlantis.[4] By doing so, he welcomes a significant amount of traditional knowledge to contribute to our understanding, and not only of the antediluvian period. Guénon himself, for example, refers to the specific Biblical

---

[2] Guénon's efforts to clarify the identity of the Atlantean tradition are to be found in *Traditional Forms and Cosmic Cycles*, compiled posthumously. He chose to use this traditional designation despite modern fantasies concerning Atlantis, fantasies which have only become more pernicious.

[3] Not only has this name been perpetuated in Mesoamerica, but Tula Indians are also known from the travels of De Soto among the Mound Builders. Hubert Howe Bancroft mentions rumors of a lost city of Tula in California. The present geography of California includes Tule Lake, the center of the Modoc world within view of Mount Shasta, although the mythologist Jeremiah Curtin reported the form "Tula" in the early 20th century; and Tolay Lake, near the ancient population center of San Francisco Bay, named for a chief Tola.

[4] *The Reign of Quantity and the Signs of the Times*, Translated by Lord Northbourne, Baltimore: Penguin, 1972, page 164.

account in a footnote: "The sixth chapter of Genesis might perhaps provide, in a symbolical form, some indications relating to the distant origins of the 'counter-initiation.'"[5] In other words, the account of the Nephilim is of primary importance in relation to the Atlantean revolt; and it is precisely this subject that has been the focus of so much speculation in recent years, which is no doubt an important sign of the times.

What concerns us is simply the literal meaning of the term "Nephilim," that is, "giants," especially since American Indian lore not only includes accounts of ancient giants, but also insists upon their wickedness. For example, Stephen Powers found accounts of such giants so persistent that he took them to refer to "some long extinct race of cannibals who were superior in power to the present race. 'To them,' he says, 'may be assigned the stone mortars found in so many parts of California, which the Indians now living here did not make.'"[6] Concerning Powers, it is important to note that he restricted his field of study to those tribes not subject to the Christianization of the Spanish Missions. It is untenable, therefore, to dismiss these legends of extinct giants as retellings of the sixth chapter of Genesis.

The same may not be said for the perspective of European Americans, however. As settlement expanded westward, belief in a vanished race of giants only gained in popularity, a belief rooted in the Bible and supported by regular reports of the uncovering of allegedly large bones. Apparently President Abraham Lincoln shared this belief, since this quote is attributed to him: "The eyes of that species of extinct giants, whose bones fill the mounds of America, have gazed on Niagara, as ours do now." In recent years, compilations of and commentary on such reports have filled

---

[5] Ibid., page
[6] Quoted in Hubert Howe Bancroft, *The Native Races, volume III: Myths and Legends*, Bancroft: San Francisco, 1882, page 547.

volumes.[7] While the consistency of such reports can hardly be ignored, the present lack of giant remains is glaring. Even so, is it unreasonable to suspect a conspiracy on the part of the early American scientific community to eliminate evidence, given its evolutionary bias against confirmations of the Book of Genesis?[8]

Leaving aside such speculations, we must recognize that the monuments and graves that were for many Americans artifacts of the antediluvian world were nothing of the sort. All such monuments – and we have in mind especially the works of the Mound Builders, the source of much of the new settlers' speculation – date to a period long after the cataclysm of Atlantis.[9] Nevertheless, this presumption accompanies the exploration of America, as is obvious in the following tale from Nelson Lee's *Three Years Among the Camanches*.

Upon asking his guide about some strange ruins, including "what appeared to have been, a church or cathedral," the author is told this "legend of the Camanches:"

> Innumerable moons ago, a race of white men, ten feet high, and far more rich and powerful than any white people now living, here inhabited a large range of country,

---

[7] Such titles include *The Ancient Giants Who Ruled America* and *Giants on Record*.

[8] Similarly, since scientists dismissed the notion of a cataclysmic flood, they only grudgingly came to accept the clear geologic evidence of such an event gathered by Harlan Bretz in the state of Washington. For an account of the work of Bretz, as well as American Indian lore relating to the Deluge, see Graham Hancock's *Magicians of the Gods* (New York: St. Martin's Press, 2015).

[9] As far as dating this cataclysm is concerned, the report from Plato suggests a date at least 11,500 years before the present. A date over 12,250 years before the present has been gleaned from Guénon's writings (Joscelyn Godwin, *Atlantis and the Cycles of Time*, Rochester: Inner Traditions, pages 306-7).

> extending from the rising to the setting sun. Their fortifications crowned the summits of the mountains, protecting their populous cities situated in the intervening valleys. They excelled every other nation which has flourished, either before or since, in all manner of cunning handicraft – were brave and warlike – ruling over the land they had wrested from its ancient possessors, with a high and haughty hand...They drove the Indians from their homes, putting them to the sword...At length, in the height of their power and glory, when they remembered justice and mercy no more, and became proud and lifted up, the Great Spirit descended from above, sweeping them with fire and deluge from the face of the earth. [10]

Of course, with medieval motifs such as "cathedral," castles, and "sword," this account even contains discernable allusions to the supposed Welsh Indians, allusions no doubt familiar to Lee's readership. Unfortunately, the confusion of elements in such tales brings obscurity rather than clarity. Above all, the vanished giants of Indian lore should not be conflated with the ancient white people, who, as we have seen, were even called "diminutive." Indeed, for the Yurok author Lucy Thompson, the wicked giants – the "Pah-pel-ene" - are a race in no way alike to the peaceful Wa-gas, with the former restricted to an earlier age than the latter; and she insists that the remnants of the age of giants are exceedingly rare.[11]

To understand the age that is in evidence upon the American landscape – that is, the period following the

---

[10] Published in 1859, pages 194-5.
[11] Op. cit., page 66.

destruction of Atlantis – we must return to René Guénon and his allusions to an Atlantean legacy:

> If we make this last reservation, it is because it seems particularly difficult to determine how, after the disappearance of Atlantis, the current coming from the West was joined with another current descending from the North and proceeding directly from the Primordial Tradition, a junction from which was to result the constitution of the different traditional forms proper to the last part of the Manvantara. This is in any case not a matter of a reabsorption pure and simple of the Primordial Tradition of what went forth from it at an earlier epoch; it is a matter of a sort of fusion of forms previously differentiated to give birth to other forms adapted to new circumstances of time and place…If one wished to research the conditions under which that fusion took place, it would doubtless be necessary to give particular importance to the Celts and the Chaldeans, whose name, which is the same, designated in reality not a particular people, but rather a sacerdotal caste; but who knows today what the Celtic and Chaldean traditions were..?[12]

To assist the one wishing to research these matters, Guénon elsewhere provides some particulars concerning the survival of Atlantean elements within these new "fusions of forms." For example, he often makes reference to the symbolism of

---

[12] "The Place of the Atlantean Tradition in the *Manvantara*" in *Traditional Forms and Cosmic Cycles*, Hillsdale: Sophia Perennis, 2003, page 26.

the bear as an emblem of the Atlantean tradition.[13] In an article focusing on the Celtic tradition, he specifies the bear as the symbol of its warrior caste; and so for these warriors, "it would seem that the part of the tradition more especially destined for them comprised above all elements proceeding from the Atlantean tradition."[14]

In light of this important observation, an oft-repeated story deriving from Joaquin Miller's *Life Amongst the Modocs* should be reconsidered.[15] The story concerns Mount Shasta as the dwelling of the Great Spirit, and it is important to note that this mountain is identified by the Shasta Indians as an ancient refuge during a great flood.[16] Its traditional name, Wyeka, signifies "white mountain," a name Guénon includes among the designations of spiritual centers.[17] According to Miller, a young daughter of the Great Spirit descends the mountain and is raised among bears; only these bears "walked on two legs, and talked, and used clubs to fight with." In time she is happily married with many children; "But, being part of the Great Spirit and part of the grizzly bear, these children did not resemble either of their parents, but partook somewhat of the nature and likeness of both. Thus was the red man created; for these children were the

---

[13] Guénon bases this observation in part on the secondary but widespread recognition of Ursa Major as a bear (see "The Wild Boar and the Bear" in *Symbols of Sacred Science*, Hillsdale: Sophia Perennis, 2004). Perhaps not surprisingly, this identification of the constellation is predominant in the American tradition.

[14] Ibid., page 164.

[15] Parts of this story appear in Bancroft's *The Native Races*, Donnelly's *Ragnarak: the Age of Fire and Gravel*, etc.

[16] Cf. Roland Dixon's "Shasta Myths" in *The Journal of American Folklore*, volume 23, number 87, January-March 1910, page 36. Despite the title of his work, Joaquin Miller lived among the Shasta Indians.

[17] René Guénon, *The King of the World*, Hillsdale: Sophia Perennis, 2001, page 64. Guénon mentions that the "white mountain" is specifically a symbol of Aztlan, the northern homeland of the Mexican peoples.

first Indians."[18] Ultimately the Great Spirit recovered his daughter and returned with her to the mountain. Leaving aside Miller's predictable poetic embellishments, his story most essentially identifies American Indian tradition as the result of a descent from a "white mountain" or spiritual center joined to a warrior society of "bears," that is, the emblem of the Atlantean tradition. That is not all, for this story even includes the ultimate withdrawal of the "white" element. No doubt all this may be compared with the foundations of traditional society described in the last chapter, with its "red" warriors and "white" spiritual authorities, as well as the ultimate disappearance of a white people.

With its memory of giants and floods and its archaeological data that suggests increasing antiquity, the American tradition is no doubt rooted in a remote and vanished "Atlantean" past. There is, however, a more recent current "descending from the North" that contained a sacerdotal dimension; it is this current that would appear to be represented by the ancient white or "Moon-eyed" people, whom the Yurok also associated with the North, as we have seen. Of course, even the disappearance or exile of this "white" aspect could not leave only Atlantean elements, as we have seen suggested by the children left following the departure of the Great Spirit's daughter in Miller's story.[19] Since the temporal is naturally "receptive" in relation to the sacerdotal, the latter would be expected to have left an imprint upon the former. Among the Cherokee, for example, the revolt against the sacerdotal caste left "priestly functions to be assumed thereafter by individual doctors and

---

[18] Hartford: American Publishing, 1874, page 274.
[19] Curiously, Lucy Thompson insists that the children of equal descent from the Wa-gas and the Yurok "with the exception of a few" left with the former, and adds (page 66): "nearly all those that were three quarters Indian remained with our people. This is said to be the reason why some of our people are very fair."

conjurors,"[20] so the consequences of this revolt relate more essentially to the question of initiatory integrity.

Following his comments concerning postdiluvian forms quoted above, Guénon continues with some remarks of particular relevance here:

> One cannot be overprudent when it comes to civilizations that have entirely disappeared, and it is certainly not the attempts at reconstitution to which profane archaeologists devote themselves that are likely to shed light on the question; but it is nonetheless true that many vestiges of a forgotten past are coming out of the earth in our age, and perhaps not without reason. Without risking the slightest prediction on what can result from these discoveries, the possible importance of which those who make them are generally incapable of suspecting, we must certainly see in this a "sign of the times."[21]

---

[20] Mooney, page 392.
[21] See note 12.

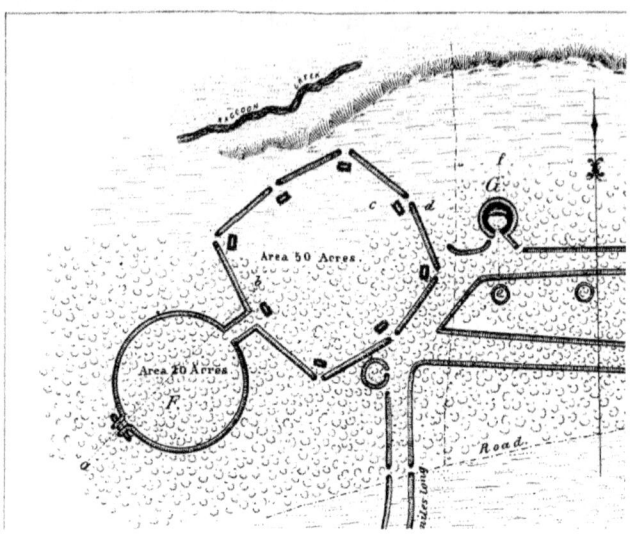

Newark Earthworks, Ohio
The octagon is oriented to the 19-year lunar standstill. According to the Sabians of Harran, the lunar temple specifically has the form of an octagon.

3

Moon Watchers

No doubt such a "sign of the times" is the recent uncovering of what had long been hidden at Göbekli Tepe. Although named a "tepe," or natural hill, the megalithic structures at this location in Turkey had been purposely buried in ancient stages within an artificial mound. Despite the "general incapacity" of the modern mentality, Göbekli Tepe has already changed minds, since the calculation of the site's extreme age immediately dispelled the false notion that the rise of religion followed the development of agriculture in Mesopotamia. The stone sanctuary at Göbekli Tepe unmistakably predates this development; in fact, the deepest levels so far unearthed have indicated dates of over 11,000 years before the present. In other words, the stones brought to light at Göbekli Tepe belong to an era that followed not long after the timing suggested above for the fall of Atlantis; and some researchers, at least, have now determined that the astrological symbolism on display in the animal carvings likely refers to catastrophic changes in the world.[1]

The temporal setting of Göbekli Tepe is especially relevant in the context of René Guénon's reference to the Chaldeans, since its geographical position is associated with that ancient tradition. Göbekli Tepe is located within the

---

[1] See Sweatman and Cooms, "Decoding European Palaeolithic Art: Extremely Ancient Knowledge of the Precession of the Equinoxes." These changes relate to what is termed by modern scientists the Younger Dryas.

district of Şanlıurfa, after the nearby city of the same name that is known as "Ur of the Chaldees" in the Bible. Since the term "Chaldean" is rooted in the earliest Mesopotamian context, its more modern specific applications need not detain us here. Due to its extreme antiquity, this site provides a remarkable glimpse of the Chaldean fusion of Atlantean and Hyperborean forms. As a result, we should not be surprised to find some indication of the Hyperborean current in evidence at Göbekli Tepe, for example in its distinctly northern orientation; [2] and no doubt subsequent Mesopotamian religion did maintain a preference for the North.

In the context of a sanctuary with carvings of an astrological character, it must be emphasized that in more recent times this region is uniquely associated with builders of astrological temples. These builders are identified in Islamic sources as Sabians, in reference to one of the various "Peoples of the Book" honored in the Qur'an;[3] but since there have been other communities known as Sabian, these are known as the Sabians of Harran, after their main city. Although it may be observed that these Harranians shared with the Sabians of Arabia a devotional focus on the sun, moon, and Venus, the Sabians of Harran constructed a temple for each of the seven traditional planets in various geometrical shapes particular to each.[4] Concerning the seven planets, it is worth keeping in mind that the lunar sphere is the nearest to the earth, and so transmits the influences of the higher spheres, just as it does the light of the sun. The Muslim scholar Al-Biruni observed that the city of Harran

---

[2] Cf. Andrew Collins, *Göbekli Tepe: Genesis of the Gods*, Rochester: Inner Traditions, 2014, page 79.

[3] See for example II, 62.

[4] Since the Harranians instructed that temples to Saturn should be in the form of the hexagon, it is very remarkable that modern astronomers have recently discovered that Saturn's "north polar vortex" appears to precisely form a hexagon.

resembled the moon and claimed that it was dedicated to the moon god.

Nevertheless, the identity of the Sabians of Harran as a People of the Book rests upon their adherence to the teachings of the antediluvian prophet Enoch or Idris, and so to a tradition predating the cataclysm of Atlantis. According to Abu Ma`shar al-Balkhi,[5] Idris was the first to build temples and the first to be called Hermes, a name that indicated a function inherited by others after the Flood. The second Hermes built the city of the Chaldeans that served as a center of philosophy, and Pythagoras belonged to his school. The third Hermes like the first lived in Egypt and taught the sciences of Hermeticism such as alchemy.[6] Many accounts relate that the first Hermes had foreknowledge of the Flood, and safeguarded his sciences through the cataclysm by various means, including in the form of carvings upon a pair of stone stelae; no doubt this is an interesting detail when considering the pairs of carved stelae within the enclosures at Göbekli Tepe. Of course, as John Michell observes, "Hermes is particularly associated with standing stone," and Michell cites the example of the Greek herm.[7]

For Jews, Christians, and Muslims, however, Harran is better known from its association with the prophet Abraham, who in the Book of Genesis left "Ur of the Chaldees" for this city.[8] The following story of Abraham in

---

[5] The various accounts concerning Hermes may be found in A. Fodor, "The Origins of the Arabic Legends of the Pyramids," *Acta Orientalia Academiae Scientarum Hungaricae*, volume 23, 1970.

[6] In keeping with this teaching, the Sabians of Harran undertook a pilgrimage to Egypt that focused on the Pyramids of Giza, since for them the artificial mountain of the "Great Pyramid" was the Tomb of Hermes.

[7] Op. cit., pages 80-1.

[8] Chapter XI.

the Qur'an, then, should be understood in the context of the Sabians of Harran:[9]

> 76. Thus did We show Abraham the kingdom of the heavens and the earth that he might be of those possessing certainty:
>
> 77. When the night grew dark upon him he beheld a star. He said: This is my Lord. But when it set, he said: I love not things that set.
>
> 78. And when he saw the moon uprising, he exclaimed: This is my Lord. But when it set, he said: Unless my Lord guide me, I surely shall become one of the folk who are astray.
>
> 79. And when he saw the sun uprising, he cried: This is my Lord! This is greater! And when it set he exclaimed: O my people! Lo! I am free from all that ye associate (with Him).
>
> 80. Lo! I have turned my face toward Him Who created the heavens and the earth, as one by nature upright, and I am not of the idolators.

Here Abraham is described as a watcher of the "kingdom of the heavens," but only in the service of monotheism to avoid deviation. The term *hanif* - translated as "one by nature upright" - traditionally identifies those naturally inclined to monotheism, and Abraham is the archetype. While Qur'anic commentary admits that some Harranians came to follow the faith of Abraham, it is very significant indeed that the term *hanif* becomes generally applied to the Sabians of Harran during the Islamic period.

The relationship between monotheism and the science of the Harranians would have been the concern of a sacerdotal authority; and there is an important indication

---

[9] Surah VI. For a proper understanding of Abraham according to traditional sources, see the recent work by Karima Sperling (*Ibrahim Khalil Allah*, Little Bird Press, 2019).

about its Chaldean formulation in the article "Seth" by René Guénon. After establishing the relationship between Nimrod and the Hebrew and Arabic names for "panther," and so with the symbolism of the Kshatriya or warrior caste, Guénon observes that "the foundation of Nineveh and of the Assyrian empire by Nimrod actually seems to have been a revolt of the Kshatriyas against the authority of the Chaldean sacerdotal caste. Thence the legendary relationship established between Nimrod and the *Nephilim* or other antediluvian "giants" which the Kshatriyas also represent in ancient times; and thence the epithet of "nimrodian" applied to a temporal power which affirms itself as independent of the spiritual authority."[10] An unmistakable connection must therefore be made between the "Chaldean sacerdotal caste" and the role of Abraham against Nimrod. Similarly, the temporal character of Harranian science becomes "nimrodian" if it is considered independent of the monotheism of Abraham.

This sacerdotal authority of Abraham no doubt relates to a curious event in the Bible in which Melchizedek appears. René Guénon in fact devotes a chapter to this mysterious Melchizedek, the "King of Salem" or "Peace," in his key work, *The King of the World*. In the Book of Genesis,[11] Melchizedek – known by a title that literally means "saint (*zedek*) king," and so indicates the union of spiritual authority and temporal power – blesses Abraham in the name of the "Most High." The superior authority of Melchizedek is further indicated by Abraham's offering of a tithe. Now, comparing these specific references to verses in the Qur'an at last reveals Melchizedek's proper identity:

> *56. And make mention in the Scripture of Idris.*
> *Lo! he was a saint (siddiq), a prophet;*
> *57. And We raised him to high station.*[12]

---

[10] *Symbols of Sacred Science*, page 134.
[11] XIV, 17-20.
[12] Surah XIX.

With Idris here named as *siddiq*, the Arabic equivalent of *zedek*, and identified with the "high," the many other correspondences with Melchizedek are easily understood, including an ever-living existence. While we have already traced antediluvian knowledges to Idris, it is important to acknowledge that the sacerdotal authority considered here is not merely antediluvian, but is rather synonymous with that "Hyperborean current" that is the proper source not only of the Atlantean tradition, but also of the "forms adapted to new circumstances" after its fall. Only the Primordial Tradition itself may be understood to be ever living in a station high above worldly tribulations.

Mention was made in passing of how the name of the Chaldean tradition is identical to that of the Celts; this suggests that the name "was not originally that of a particular people, but of a sacerdotal caste, exercising spiritual authority among different peoples."[13] No doubt Abraham, associated above with the Chaldean tradition, is considered the father of many nations; yet it is to the original function of Abraham, and not to the claims of particular peoples, that the Qur'an refers:

> *Abraham was not a Jew, nor yet a Christian; but he was an upright man (hanif) who had surrendered (to Allah), and he was not of the idolaters.*[14]

The sacerdotal castes of various "barbarous nations" were named by Clement of Alexandria: "Philosophy, then, with all its blessed advantages to man, flourished long ages ago among the barbarians, diffusing its light among the gentiles, and eventually penetrated into Greece. Its hierophants were

---

[13] René Guénon, "The Wild Boar and the Bear," ibid., page 162, footnote 17.
[14] III, 67.

the prophets among the Egyptians, the Chaldeans among the Assyrians, the Druids among the Galatians, the Sramanas of the Bactrians[15], and the philosophers of the Celts, the Magi among the Persians who announced beforehand the birth of the Saviour, being led by a star till they arrived in the land of Judea, and among the Indians the Gymnosophists."[16] Not only does this list bring together the Chaldeans and Celts, but Abraham also has a relationship with the "Gymnosophists" or Brahmin caste of India. Given that the name "Brahma" is so similar to Abraham, it is not surprising that the great master of Islamic esoterism ʿAbdul-Karim al-Jili identifies the tradition of the Brahmins – at least in its metaphysical formulation, free of idolatry - with the Abrahamic heritage.[17]

By a curious historical "accident," the American tradition is likewise known by the designation "Indian;" but is a deeper association with these other forms so unthinkable?[18] In 1866, in the context of "Indian Secret Societies," the similarities between the Cherokee Aní-Kutání and the Brahmins of India were clear enough to point out.[19] Modern research is only beginning to admit the celestial alignments of American ruins from Cahokia to Chaco, and no one has bothered to consider their Sabian resonance. The constructions of the Mound Builders are alternatively geometrical, recalling the Harranian temples, or in the form of animals with celestial correspondences that recall the

---

[15] These are in all likelihood Buddhists.

[16] *Stromata* 1. In presenting his evidence for the Hyperborean current in *The Arctic Home in the Vedas*, Tilak depends primarily on sources belonging to the last two traditions in this list.

[17] *Al-Insan al-kamil*, chapter 63.

[18] Guénon mentions in passing the similarity between Vedic rites and what is called "shamanism," in the context of how primitive animism properly belongs to the Primordial Tradition (op. cit. 1972, chapter XXVI). On the relationship of the final Abrahamic tradition with shamanism, cf. *Shamanism and Islam*, edited by Zarcone and Hobart, London: I.B. Taurus, 2013.

[19] Fogelson, page 256.

carvings at Göbekli Tepe; and the descendants of the culture responsible for them may perhaps best be described as "naturally inclined to monotheism." As for the name "Moon-eyed People," it is only reasonable to consider that this curious designation identifies people who watch the heavens, at the very least, and it follows that the monuments "on the tops of high mountains and places commanding a view" may very well relate to astronomical observation, recalling the focus of the Magi. Moreover, a remarkable assertion of the present-day Cherokee suggests part of the teaching of this "white" caste: "Before the Trail of Tears, when the Cherokee were forced to leave their land, their villages were built to reflect the shape of a particular constellation, so profound was their understanding of their place in the universe."[20]

If indications of a relationship with Mesopotamia seem too remote, we should consider a remarkable artifact kept but not displayed at the oldest museum of the United States Army, at West Point. Upon the surrender of the great peacemaker Chief Joseph of the Nez Perce in 1877, following a display of strategic mastery in eluding capture as his people were pursued over a thousand miles, found among the contents of his medicine bag was a small clay tablet. Originally called a Nez Perce "pictograph," its inscription is actually cuneiform, and its provenance is unquestionably Mesopotamian.[21] Lacking an explanation from Chief Joseph, speculation has come to obscure the truth somewhat, yet still the tablet's mundane inscription serves to provide a date of some 4000 years ago, thanks to its reference to a temple of the Harranians' moon god. No doubt the mundane character of

---

[20] Quoted in Ross Hamilton, *Star Mounds: Legacy of a Native American Mystery*, Berkeley: North Atlantic Books, 2012, page 20. Hamilton's work is indebted to the vision of the "traditional philosopher" John Michell.

[21] An accurate account of its provenance – along with a feeble attempt to invent an alternate explanation for its presence in the museum - may be found in the *Smithsonian* magazine of February 1979.

this artifact is itself an argument for its authenticity, unlike so many other "proofs" of pre-Columbian contact that have plagued American archaeology; and its date is as near as might be ventured for the time of Abraham.

The tablet of Chief Joseph

The Red and the White

Mount Shasta

4

People of the Mounds

Along with the erroneous identification as a natural hill, the megalithic sanctuary near "Ur of the Chaldees" has been given the name "potbelly" ("göbekli"). Now, while this word may simply describe the appearance of its ancient mound, it is nevertheless an important one, given the meaning of the word omphalos - "navel" - that identifies a geomantic center. The term omphalos is Greek, and is applied above all to the center of the Greek world at Delphi, or more exactly to its sacred stone. Like such a stone or stone pillar, a central mound may serve as a substitute for the polar mountain, the primordial formulation of the axis linking worlds above and below.[1] We have already mentioned an American polar mountain in Mount Shasta, and it should come as no surprise that the constructions of the Mound Builders should dominate a landscape where mountains are not already in evidence. We have also seen that the ancient white people were associated with the building of these mounds, but at the same time, we should note that stories of the ancient white people are perhaps best known among peoples living in relative proximity to Mount Shasta.

The primordial emblem of the swastika, signifying the activity of the central principle upon this world, is in fact one of the primary symbols of the Mound Builders. Obviously this emblem is known above all from its use in India, hence its Sanskrit name. Another important emblem of

---

[1] For the best study of this symbolism see Guénon's *The King of the World*.

the Mound Builders, the Water Panther, is a curious one. To begin with, the Water Panther and the Horned Serpent seem to be variants of the same motif in traditional American cosmology, and often enough a hybrid form appears; even so, the ubiquity of this underworld figure throughout America – along with its opposite, the Thunderbird - indicates that despite differences of language and custom, the American tradition is essentially singular. That is not all, since the Horned Serpent belongs likewise to the Celtic and Mesopotamian cosmologies; and it is the strange insistence on an underwater "panther" that betrays the very particularly nimrodian significance of this formulation. [2]

Of course, the sanctuary at Delphi was only renewed by Apollo's slaying of the underworld serpent Python.[3] Remarkably, it was through the patronage of the Pythian Apollo that this center of the Classical world was linked to Hyperborea, since Apollo was believed to travel by swan to Hyperborea and spend every winter there. However, an alternate account has his regular visit undertaken every nineteen years. Now, nineteen is a number that refers specifically to the cycle of the moon; and while Apollo is associated traditionally with the sun, he is properly not the sun god (who is Helios) but rather the god of light, and his Hyperborean association places him in the context of a polar symbolism that has priority over the solar. Moreover, a preference for lunar rather than solar observation pertains to lands located further to the north, as Alexander Thom has shown in his researches in Britain.

Perhaps not surprisingly, Classical authorities consistently conflate the Celts of northern lands with Hyperboreans. This is obviously imprecise, since the Celtic

---

[2] The Water Panther may also be profitably compared to the Questing Beast of the Celtic Arthurian cycle, especially since the Questing Beast with its composite form is also associated with water.

[3] The center of the Nez Perce world is a mound known as the Heart of the Monster, and commemorates a similar victory.

tradition represents rather a fusion of Atlantean and Hyperborean currents. Indeed, within Celtic mythology itself may be found a clear reference to this fusion, embodied in the Tuatha Dé Danann of Ireland. According to accounts of the island's ancient invasions, these descendants of a legendary chief are described as arriving in "clouds" upon the mountains to inherit the sovereignty of Ireland. Prior to their arrival, the Tuatha Dé Danann were said to have traveled to four islands in the North where they had acquired learning in arcane arts, and here is a clear indication of Hyperborea.[4] Their mythological rule was marked by conflict with the Fomorians, dark giants with whom they nevertheless could marry, and who recall in some manner the Atlantean tradition. A final invasion of Ireland brought the Milesians - from the Latin *miles* or "soldier" – who came to supplant the Tuatha Dé Danann in turn. More exactly, the two groups entered into a strange arrangement: the Milesians would rule the land above the surface, while the Tuatha Dé Danann would rule an unseen world below. Nevertheless, heroes of Irish legend afterwards could receive supernatural assistance from their enchanted realm.

This retreat of Hyperborean representatives to the unseen recalls a development described by René Guénon in the chapter "The Supreme Center Concealed during the Kali-Yuga" in *The King of the World*. This development may also be compared to the disappearance of the ancient white people according to Lucy Thompson, except that she describes their return to their supreme country in the North; it is no doubt significant that she also describes worthy Yuroks being taken there by supernatural birds, recalling the flight of the Pythian Apollo as well as the cloud-borne arrival of the Tuatha Dé Danann. However, it must be recognized that the more popular understanding of the Yurok to this day is that the

---

[4] Just as four rivers belong to Paradise, so too does the Hyperborean center in this case have four islands and four cities, each with its own specialty in the arcane arts.

Wo'gey long ago hid themselves in myriad special places in the landscape, and "many of the spirit-persons went into the upper ridges to live, and this is why Indians traditionally go to the high country to make medicine."[5] The parallel with the Tuatha Dé Danann becomes even more obvious, and again reflects the "ever-living" nature of the Primordial Tradition.

However, a further development in Celtic folklore must be addressed, namely that the subterranean Tuatha Dé Danann have become equated with the "People of the Mounds (*Aos sí*)," that is, the elves or fairies. Of course, given their ubiquity in folklore worldwide, it may not be surprising that such creatures are recognized in American Indian lore.[6] Such lore has in fact been compiled by a National Park Service ranger in the volume *American Elves*, and the Wo'gey are included therein. In other words, the supernatural character of an ancient people has led to their being grouped among creatures who are not human, and who, in both the Celtic and American Indian examples, appear as "little people." This is, in addition to their pacifism, the likely reason for the ancient white people being described as diminutive; Thompson, however, does not describe them as such. In fact, in *American Elves*, we find the following entry: "Chetco *woge* were small, white, and pacifist, but Hupa Kikunnai and Tolowa white woge or waug appear to be human-sized."[7] Moreover, one of the Yurok informants of the anthropologist Alfred Kroeber described the Wo'gey as "large men:" "They wore elk skins and these were like small blankets, so big were the men."[8] Another academic following Kroeber offers that "Indian persons whom I interviewed said that they were not necessarily small but 'just different.'"[9]

---

[5] Keeling, page 57.

[6] In fact, on their journey to the West, Lewis and Clark were shown an isolated symmetrical hill that was recognized by the Maha Indians as belonging to the "Little People."

[7] John Roth, *American Elves*, Jefferson: McFarland, 1997, page 120.

[8] *Yurok Myths*, University of California Press, 1976, page 178.

[9] Keeling, page 56.

This confusion of an absent spiritual authority with the unseen world of the elves is perhaps understandable, but it is nevertheless problematic. It has proven to be a persistent problem, as evidenced by the fact that the modern popular conception of angels hardly differs from that of beautiful fairies, whereas the very existence of fairies is not easily substantiated by the Bible. In Christian folklore, however, elves or fairies have been identified as "fallen angels," or more leniently with "neutral angels" who sided neither with the Heavenly Host nor with the fallen.

The Qur'anic revelation is rather more clear on such matters. It is, after all, addressed not only to humanity, but also to the world of unseen creatures called jinn. While not neutral, the jinn do in a sense occupy a rank between the angels and humanity; and like the latter, the jinn are able to choose between good and evil. Since Lucifer is moreover identified as one of the jinn,[10] those who fell are not identified as angels at all, since the latter are understood by their luminous nature to be infallible. In any case, fairies may naturally be seen to belong to the jinn,[11] and so to a different ontological degree than either angels or human beings.

These three creatures – angels, jinn, and human – in some measure embody the traditional division of the cosmos into three degrees: the spiritual, psychic, and corporeal.[12] Yet the human being is in the traditional conception the microcosm, and so contains all three degrees as spirit, soul, and body; and it follows that the constitution of a human tradition would contain all three elements, and the sacerdotal castes that we have been considering obviously relate to the spiritual degree.

---

[10] *Qur'an* XVIII, 50.

[11] In this connection, it may be offered that the identification of the Nephilim as "fallen angels" according to the apocryphal Book of Enoch should rather be interpreted as referring to the jinn.

[12] These three worlds are comparable to the sky world, the underworld, and the earth in American Indian cosmology.

Yet here we are concerned not merely with the concealment of a spiritual authority, but more importantly its reduction to something fay, and René Guénon has in fact addressed such a possibility. In the chapter "Psychic Residues" of his magnum opus, *The Reign of Quantity and the Signs of the Times,* Guénon mentions the comparison between a tradition and the human microcosm, and continues:

> Comparisons of this kind can only be fully understood if it is remembered that even spiritual influences themselves must necessarily, if they are to come into action in our world, take appropriate "supports," first of all in the psychic order, then in the corporeal order itself, so that the result is something analogous to the constitution of a human being. If later on the spiritual influences for any reason withdraw themselves, their former corporeal supports, whether places or objects (and when places are in question their situation is naturally connected with the "sacred geography" mentioned earlier) will none the less remain charged with psychic elements which will be all the stronger and more persistent for having served as the intermediaries and the instruments of a yet more powerful action.

Guénon goes on to warn of the dangers attached to "certain vestiges of ancient civilizations, when they come to be exhumed by people who, like the modern archaeologists, know nothing of such matters, and so inevitably fail to act with prudence."[13] So it is hardly suspected that the reason for the deliberate burial of Göbekli Tepe has something to do with "protective measures," or rather a sacerdotal defense

---

[13] Op. cit., pages 221-2.

against such psychic residues.[14] The Navajo people, however, are very much aware of such matters. Not only does their cosmology account for the ghosts of the past, but they moreover believed that in certain cases "strong rituals were needed to keep them 'beaten into the ground.'" The Navajo perspective on scientific exhumation has been described in this way: "to disturb something that was physically buried in the deep past, and bring it into the present, unravels the densely woven net of time – in effect, it breaches the barrier of time – and that will have undesirable consequences."[15]

Following the withdrawal of the spirit of a tradition, another method of safeguarding against disturbances must be to restore a spiritual presence to a place. An example is to be found at Luxor in Egypt, where sands had buried its temple of Amun before the saint Abul-Hajjaj came to be interred in its upper reaches; when Egyptian authorities in modern times excavated the complex to promote tourism, the saint nevertheless remained unmoved. Another example is at Nineveh, where the tomb of Jonah has been situated atop an artificial mound of extreme antiquity, and so its inviolability was acknowledged by the three so-called Abrahamic traditions. Of course, the saintly presence at such places provides a focus for the performance of "strong rituals."[16]

A location especially worth considering in the Celtic context is a shrine of the Seven Sleepers of Ephesus at Vieux-Marché in Brittany. This Roman Catholic chapel was established early in the Christian history of France within an ancient megalithic dolmen. Now, as the Orientalist Louis Massignon has demonstrated, the veneration of the Seven Sleepers of Ephesus belongs both to Christianity and Islam

---

[14] Indeed other locations come to mind in this regard, such as the very ancient sanctuary in Orkney at the extreme north of Britain.
[15] Adrienne Mayor, *Fossil Legends of the First Americans*, Princeton: Princeton University Press, 2005, page 131-3.
[16] Even though what had been buried deep within Göbekli Tepe had seemingly been forgotten, the sanctity of the hill was still recognized in modern times, owing to a small cemetery upon its summit.

and so possesses an Abrahamic significance also;[17] and it was through an annual pilgrimage to this shrine that Massignon personally brought into practice his aim of reconciling Christians and Muslims. The Qur'anic commentator al-Qashani explains the role of the Seven Sleepers: "Know that the Companions of the Cave are the seven saints charged with preserving the Divine Order in the world: it only subsists through them. They remain at all times according to the number and the hierarchy of the planets." Here it is worth mentioning that the Qur'anic account of their story [18] describes a northern orientation for the cave, and names the Companions as "knights." Massignon provides a list in his work of the very many shrines in many lands dedicated to them, and it is noteworthy that the lands of Britain are not included; but given their designation as knights, it should be recognized that the several locations in Britain where King Arthur and his companions are reportedly sleeping underground serve as worthy substitutes.[19]

This last observation includes an unavoidable promise, since Arthur is the "Once and Future King." Despite their disappearance, the representatives of the Primordial

---

[17] "Le Culte Liturgique et Populaire des VII Dormants Martyrs d'Ephese (Ahl al-Kahf): Traite d'Union Orient-Occident entre l'Islam et la Chretiente."

[18] XVIII, 9-22.

[19] On the matter of the reconciliation of Christianity and Islam in the Arthurian context, please see *L'Islam et le Graal* by Pierre Ponsoye (Milan: Arche, 1976). According to the *Queste del Saint Graal*, the wizard Merlin constructed the Round Table in reference to the sky, and so the knights of Arthur may be understood to partake in the planetary symbolism of the Companions of the Cave. Indeed, it is through the guidance of the Celtic Merlin that the power of Arthur – whose name means "bear" – is sanctioned. The Round Table itself may be compared to the many stone circles that refer to the celestial bodies, including the "medicine wheel" of the American tradition. A comparative study of a North American medicine wheel and the most famous stone circle has been undertaken by Gordon R. Freeman, entitled *Hidden Stonehenge*.

Tradition are expected to return, as the story of the awakening Companions of the Cave makes clear.[20] For her part, Lucy Thompson does not fail to mention this promise in her account of the disappearance of the ancient white people: "Some of the Indians are still looking for their return to the earth, when they come back it is believed that peace and happiness will reign supreme again over this great land and all evil will be cast out."[21]

---

[20] Curiously, since accounts of the Seven Sleepers attribute the discovery of their awakening to the use of unusual currency, a modern account of a race hiding within Mount Shasta includes such a motif (Wishar S. Cervé, *Lemuria: Lost Continent of the Pacific*, AMORC, 1997, page 178). In most every other respect, however, claims about this race of "Lemurians" from a submerged land suggest that they belong rather to the category of "psychic residues." After all, though it is strangely never mentioned, the very name "Lemurian" properly refers to the dangerous spirits of the dead in ancient Rome. The name of their city Telos, then, appears to be a parody of Tula. Still, the very presence of these residues is yet another indication that Mount Shasta once served as an important spiritual center in traditional America; and for Richard L. Tierney, even the modern legends of Mount Shasta resemble nothing more than Muslim lore with its "'white-robed saints.'" ("America's Mystical Mount Shasta," *Fate*, Highland Park: Clark Publishing, vol. 36, no. 8, issue 401, August 1983).

[21] Op. cit., page 66.

World Renewal Ceremony
Initiates of the White Deerskin Dance, c. 1900

5

Fixing the Earth

Concerning the mound at Nineveh, it was precisely its Abrahamic sanctification that made it a target of the nimrodian agents of the Counter-tradition, who under the guise of an "Islamic State" violated this sanctuary in 2014. Indeed, the rise of I.S.I.S. itself may relate to psychic residues belonging specifically to the landscape of modern Iraq, and these residues may be "all the stronger" due to the power of its ancient tradition; and this was made possible since, as "Wahhabis," the followers of I.S.I.S. have cut themselves off from the spirituality of Islam. In any case, one of the policies of I.S.I.S. had been to mark the houses of Christians with the first letter of the Arabic word for "Christian" (*nasarah*), and in response, Muslims declaring their opposition to I.S.I.S. adopted this letter Nūn as the sign of their solidarity with the Christians of Iraq.[1]

What is truly remarkable is that the Qur'anic designation of the prophet Jonah, whose tomb was violated at Ninevah, is Dhul-Nūn, the "Lord" or "Owner of Nūn," that is, the very same Arabic letter. Of course, since the name of the letter is also a name for a fish, the story of this prophet being swallowed by the whale or fish is clearly indicated here. However, there is a strange saying of Jesus reported in the Gospels that should be recalled: "An evil and adulterous

---

[1] It is important to note that this development originally signaled a bringing together of Muslims and Christians, even though the support of Christian factions internationally would seem to have eclipsed this original formulation.

generation seeketh after a sign; and there shall be no sign given to it, but the sign of the prophet Jonas."[2] In the light of the Qur'anic revelation, this "sign" is none other than the Nūn, and the saying of Jesus has only been made clear by recent events.[3]

The word Nūn does not merely refer to any fish, but signifies particularly the cosmic creature of the waters that upholds the world in Islamic cosmology: "He created the earth upon a big fish, that being the fish (*nūn*) mentioned by God in the Qur'an: *"Nūn. By the Pen."* [4] This Nūn may therefore be compared to another aquatic creature, the turtle, which has the analogous role in the context of both the Indian *and* American Indian cosmologies. In fact, the shape of the Arabic letter, a matter of tremendous interest to masters of Islamic esoterism from Shaykh Muhyiddin Ibn 'Arabi to René Guénon, shares in this comparison. The letter Nūn is essentially the lower part of the circumference of a circle, with the center of this circle marked by a dot; and this dot establishes the presence of a hidden, superior half-circumference, that is the "spiritual" Nūn:" [5]

---

[2] Matthew XII, 39.

[3] It would be relevant here to consider the Arthurian theme of the Fisher King, but this would bring us too far away from our subject.

[4] *The History of al-Tabari, Volume 1: General Introduction and From the Creation to the Flood*, translated by Franz Rosenthal, Albany: SUNY Press, 1989, page 220.

[5] See Denis Gril, "The Science of Letters," in Ibn al 'Arabi, *The Meccan Revelations Volume II*, edited by Michel Chodkiewicz, New York: Pir Press, 2004.

Fixing the Earth

These two separate parts correspond remarkably well with the carapace and plastron of the turtle. In any case, when completed as a circle with a central point, the two forms of the Nūn become equivalent to the Ojibwe hieroglyph for "spirit."

In addition, there is another context where both forms of the Nūn appear in traditional America. In the Southwest, the Hopi people once included a group known as the "Moon Clan;" and though this clan is considered extinct, these are the petroglyphs associated with it: [6]

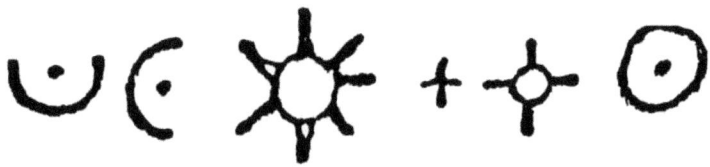

Here are to be identified astrological symbols, and, of course, the form of the Arabic letter. In keeping with the designation "Moon Clan," a particularly lunar significance emerges when considering the four lines of a cross alongside a circle with seven rays, since the monthly cycle of the moon may be naturally divided into four phases of seven days' duration. The total number of days – 28 – is the number of the lunar mansions, and features in the structure of the circular "medicine wheels" and certain sacred lodges of the Plains Indians.

Returning to the significance of the Arabic letter and the Islamic understanding of the cosmic fish, the position of the earth upon it was naturally unstable:

---

[6] Alex Patterson, *A Field Guide to Rock Art Symbols of the Greater Southwest*, Boulder: Johnson Books, page 147.

> The fish moved and became agitated. As a result, the earth quaked, whereupon He firmly anchored the mountains on it, and it was stable...This is stated in God's word that He made for the earth *"firmly anchored (mountains), lest it shake you up."*[7]

This role of the mountains in balancing the world may be compared with the traditional understanding of Mount Shasta. For the Achomawi Indians, the spirit within the mountain "balances the earth with the universe and the universe with the earth."[8] In the Qur'an, this balancing function has been designated by a specific term: "*And the mountains: stakes.*"[9] Now, "stakes" (*awtad*) has in turn been applied to four holy personages at the summit of the spiritual hierarchy, whose function has been explained in the writings of the Shaykh Muhyiddin Ibn `Arabi. At the highest cosmic level these four are identified as the four ever-living prophets: Idris, Jesus, Elijah, and the one known as al-Khidr, the "Green Man." The cosmological role of the Awtad may be compared to the four sacred mountains that establish the world of the Navajo people; and given the relevance of the cosmic turtle, their role may also be perceived in the Chinese myth of Nüwa removing the four legs of a sea tortoise in order to hold up the sky. What is more, the Chinese character for a Taoist saint – *xian* – signifies literally "human mountain."

The leader of the four Awtad is Idris, who was associated above with the "Hyperborean current;" in Islamic

---

[7] Al-Tabari, page 220.

[8] Darryl Babe Wilson, "Mis Misa: The Power within Akoo-Yet that Protects the World," *Native American Voices*, New York: Routledge, 2010, page 56.

[9] LXXVIII, 7. This correspondence of mountain and stake finds expression in the Great Spirit "boring a hole in the sky, using a great stone as an augur" to create Mount Shasta according to a myth of the Shasta Indians related by Bancroft (op. cit., page 91).

civilization, doctors and geomancers alike are under his patronage. As we have already explained, Melchizedek is but a title of Idris, and so we should recall that Jesus is identified in the Book of Hebrews as a "priest forever after the order of Melchizedek," a reference that must indicate this specific rank of the spiritual hierarchy. Of course, Jesus has also long been associated with the fish in Christianity, though a proper understanding of this is usually reduced to an acronym; he is also associated with "living waters."[10] Another of the Awtad, the mysterious figure known as al-Khidr [11] is traditionally depicted in Islamic miniature paintings standing securely upon a fish as it moves through the waters, clearly in reference to this spiritual rank. According to Charles-André Gilis, who along with his master Michel Vâlsan are to be considered the only proper continuators of the work of René Guénon, the four Awtad may be understood to represent specific dimensions of authority: Jesus represents sacerdotal authority, Idris royal power, and Elijah and al-Khidr the double cosmic force corresponding to the *solve* and *coagula* of Hermeticism.[12]

This last insight is especially valuable, since it helps to explain the strange yet balanced way in which these two prophets appear in Islamic cultures. To begin with, the association of al-Khidr and Elijah (Ilyas) is so close that their names are run together in the name of the spring festival of the Ottoman Empire, "Hidrellez." In the Ottoman *Saltikname*, the two prophets appear as brothers of the same mother. In

---

[10] Cf. John VII, 38: "He that believeth on me, as the scripture hath said, out of his belly shall flow rivers of living water." The use of the word "belly" here recalls the meaning of omphalos.

[11] It is no doubt of interest that al-Jili describes a "region in the North, never reached by any sinner, which is ruled by al-Khadir and inhabited by the Men of the Unseen World." (R. A. Nicholson, *Studies in Islamic Mysticism*, Cambridge: Cambridge University Press, 1978, page 124)

[12] Abd ar-Razzâq Yahyâ, *Le Maître de l'Or*, Paris: Le Turban Noir, 2016, page 21.

the epic accounts of Alexander the Great, details concerning them are variable, yet they are as a rule depicted in miniature paintings together at the Water of Life. It is also believed that they meet in their nightly rounds at the Wall of Alexander, the construction of which is described in the Qur'an[13] and that serves as the archetype of a cosmic "protective measure" against very dangerous elements indeed. What is more, they provide help to those in distress, on land or at sea; and even though al-Khidr is most often associated with water, he is said to be the helper on land, and while Elijah is remembered for his fiery ascent to Heaven, he is said to be the helper at sea. In this context, and given the Hermetic character of standing stones that was mentioned above, it is worth considering that the twin pillars at Göbekli Tepe may likewise represent a balancing of Hermeticism's "double cosmic force."

To understand the relevance of all this to our subject, we must recognize that below the level of the ever-living prophets, there are others in more relative domains who, during their lifetimes, are considered to represent and act on behalf of these four, and they are also considered Awtad. Given the correspondence of these saints with mountains, we should recall that the Yuroks go to the mountains "to make medicine," and the need for the medicine bequeathed by the ancient white people is moreover based upon a traditional conception of "balance."[14]

> ...The river flooded, the earth shook, and diseases began to spread.
> There was always a struggle to keep the earth balanced upon the waters, in accord with the law and despite human breaches of it. Knowing that this would be so, before they left the *wo-gey* instructed certain people

---

[13] XVIII, 92-98.
[14] "Yurok call the balancing of dualities Wogi." (Roth, page 14)

in what to do to put the world back in balance when the weight of human violations grew too great for it. The instructions were the basis of the "world renewal cult" and of its central ritual and ceremonial occasions, the "great dances," *helomey* - jump dances and deerskin dances... Kroeber called the hereditary spiritual experts who were responsible for the dances' ritual dimensions "priests" or "formulists." Today they are called "medicine men" but in Yurok they are the ones who "talk to the world" and also "the doctors of the world;" in Karuk[15], they are the ones who "fix the world." They recite mythic narratives about the first dances, quoting the First People's speeches and, in some dances, performing acts of power that these *wo-gey* had prescribed. When they pray in this way, they use a special, ritual register of Yurok, *wo-gey* speech, in which they spoke from a *wo-gey* perspective...In effect, the medicine men become the *wo-gey*, uniting their time and form with those of the First People in the purity of the beginning through language

---

[15] Although representing a different language group according to the ethnologists, the Karuk or "upriver" people share these dances with the Yurok, or "downriver" people. The ancient white people are called *Ikhareyev* by the Karuk. In his account of "A Karuk World-Renewal Ceremony at Panaminik," Philip Drucker mentions an example of moon-watching that also significantly describes its context: "The priest observed the moon and then timed the beginning of his fast so that the ceremony would come to an end on the night of the first new moon in the month okwakos (about September)." (University of California Publications in American Archaeology and Ethnology, volume 35, number 3, January 1936, page 23)

> and asceticism. Doing this, they gain the power to return the world itself to its original condition.[16]

By replacing the word "original" with "primordial," the role of the Awtad is easily recalled, and in relation to the designation "doctors," none other than the chief of the Awtad is regarded in Islamic civilization as the doctor *par excellence*. It may very well be that, despite their disappearance, the ancient white people still exist in the American West, represented by those doctors who have the power to "fix" the earth; and their methods are doubtless akin to the "strong rituals" mentioned in the context of the Navajo.

Even so, it has become all too apparent that the delicate balance of the natural world is facing an unprecedented "weight of human violations." To provide but one small but significant example, the process of fracking elicits a convulsive response from the earth itself, and so these manmade earthquakes are an unsettling mockery of the duties of the Awtad. The disequilibrium resulting from the modern world has been given the catchphrase "climate change," and America remains unapologetic for its role in it. One voice at least offers modern people a way towards restoring that equilibrium, and it belongs to HRH the Prince of Wales. In his veritable manifesto *Harmony: A New Way of Looking at Our World*, the prince explains that the present crisis may only be understood in relation to humanity's loss of traditional wisdom.[17]

The domain of nature is traditionally understood to belong to the sublunary realm, and so the cycles of nature have a special relationship with the moon.[18] In his defense of

---

[16] Buckley, page 214-5.

[17] New York: HarperCollins, 2010.

[18] "The pull of the Moon is considerable. Not only does it move tides twice a day, it pulls on the Earth. Many gardeners and farmers are rediscovering the benefit of planting according to its phases, part of

Fixing the Earth

nature, the Prince has presented the best ways to confront the increasing threat with particular reference to the Islamic perspective, resulting in alarmist headlines: "'Follow the Islamic Way' to Save the World, Prince Charles Urges Environmentalists."[19] Yet this is perfectly in keeping with a traditional astrological perspective, according to which the religion of Islam corresponds to the moon among the planets.[20] Moreover, there is an unmistakably Abrahamic resonance in the Christian voice of the prince transmitting wisdom from the world of Islam.

In his speech "Islam and the Environment" that gave rise to the headlines, HRH the Prince of Wales reminds us:

> The Qur'an is considered to be the "last Revelation" but it clearly acknowledges which book is the first. That book is the great book of creation, of Nature herself, which has been taken too much for granted in our modern world and needs to be restored to its original position.[21]

---

a profound knowledge neglected by modern techniques." (ibid., page 137)

[19] *The Daily Mail*, 9 June 2010.

[20] Of course, it is also no accident that the crescent popularly serves as a symbol of Islam.

[21] Speech given at the Sheldonian Theatre, University of Oxford, 9 June 2010. The Shakespearean epigraph to *Harmony* concerns this "Book of Nature" very precisely; and René Guénon presents a teaching of Shaykh Muhyiddin Ibn `Arabi on this subject in *The Symbolism of the Cross* (London: Luzac and Company, 1975, page 68).

The Gottville Rain Rock
Precisely seven cupules retain water from spring rains, reflecting the
"Great Bear in the Sky"

6

Stones of Exile

Despite the disappearance of the Tuatha Dé Danann, there yet remains a cherished relic associated with the source of their authority. Some accounts describe four treasures brought from the North, one from each of the four islands, but the first recension of *Lebor Gabála* mentions only one: the Lia Fáil or Stone of Destiny.[1] This stone becomes a "speaking stone" when it serves as the coronation stone of the Celtic High Kings; the Lia Fáil therefore expresses sacerdotal sanction for legitimate royal authority. The movement of this relic may be traced from Ireland to Scotland to England, although what is popularly considered the Stone of Destiny is currently housed in Edinburgh. In its travels through Christian lands, however, an alternate origin was provided for the stone, and it became identified as the pillow of Jacob from chapter 28 of the Book of Genesis:

> 10. And Jacob went out from Beersheba, and went toward Haran.
> 11. And he Lighted upon a certain place, and tarried there all night, because the sun was set; and he took of the stones of that place, and put them for his pillows, and lay down in that place to sleep.

---

[1] It is of surely significant that the forms of these four treasures – stone, sword, spear, and basin – reappear at the heart of the Grail legends.

> 12. And he dreamed, and behold a ladder set up on the earth, and the top of it reached to heaven: and behold the angels of God ascending and descending on it.

Very remarkably, this alternate origin indicates a specifically Harranian provenance. What is more, the Biblical account provides an Abrahamic formulation of a stone omphalos:

> 18. And Jacob rose up early in the morning, and took the stone that he had put for his pillows, and set it up for a pillar, and poured oil upon the top of it.
> 19. And he called the name of that place Bethel...

In the Abrahamic tradition of Islam, the angelic ladder beheld by Jacob is known as the *mi`raj*, upon which the Prophet Muhammad is believed to have traveled during his miraculous "Night Journey and Ascension." On that night, the Prophet was welcomed to the Heavenly spheres by his prophetic predecessors, with each planetary sphere being under the spiritual authority of a prophet. In particular, Saturn was shown to be the domain of Abraham.[2] Now, Saturn is also Kronos, whose association with time accounts for both a beneficent aspect, since he was ruler of the Golden Age,[3] as well as a malefic one. In the latter aspect, he is

---

[2] In the Western formulation of the Seven Liberal Arts, each art corresponds to a planet, and the art corresponding to Saturn is astrology. This only serves to reinforce the association between the ancient white people and astrological knowledge.

[3] Guénon places Kronos in the Hyperborean context, and explains that the root k-r-n refers to elevation, with this meaning being preserved by the word cairn (see "The Symbolism of Horns" in *Symbols of Sacred Science*). In this connection, it is worth recalling the "landmarks of stone monuments, on the tops of high mountains" mentioned by Lucy Thompson.

remembered for having sought to devour his son, but through a ruse a stone was offered to him instead, and it is this very stone that becomes the Greek omphalos.[4]

Here again we find the omphalos in an Abrahamic context, and in fact the veneration of sacred stones was of central importance among the Arab descendants of Abraham in the pre-Islamic past. Of course, it is widely assumed that the Black Stone of Islam is a meteorite venerated in the pre-Islamic period; but even on a materialistic level this is unreasonable, since its fractured condition is not in keeping with a meteoric origin, nor is its distinctive characteristic of staying afloat in water. Still, the Black Stone has an indisputably Abrahamic context in the Islamic tradition, even though its origin is traced back before the Flood to the Heavenly House established in Arabia that served as the first temple on earth. Although this temple was ultimately removed to its Heavenly position, the Black Stone, originally white, remained on earth, and was shielded during the Deluge by the mountain of Abu Qubays. At the proper time, the Black Stone would come to be situated at the corner of the temple constructed in place of the Heavenly one, and it is none other than Abraham and his son Ishmael who are remembered as its builders.[5] Like the Lia Fáil, the Black Stone is believed to have a tongue with which to speak, as well as

---

[4] Strangely, Abraham is also remembered for attempting to sacrifice his son, although in this case a ram served as a mercifully mandated substitution. Cf. Sperling, chapter 41.

[5] In this cooperation of Abraham and his son, Charles-André Gilis has perceived an expression of the fusion of Hyperborean and Atlantean elements being considered here, especially since Abraham as spiritual authority is held to have flown on his mount Buraq from the direction of the North to rejoin his son, who is described in the Book of Genesis in warrior terms (see *La Doctrine Initiatique du Pèlerinage*, Paris: Les Editions de l' Œvre, 1982, pages 87-89). Strangely, this northern direction is specified with reference to Armenia, a name historically linked to the environs of Göbekli Tepe.

eyes.[6] It remains the focal point of the prayers of the faithful throughout the world surrounding it, a living visitor from Paradise.

The first Heavenly temple may be understood to embody the supra-human character of the Primordial Tradition. The temple constructed in its place serves to preserve that tradition, and indeed, Islamic esoterism maintains that the saintly Awtad correspond to its corners, and through this orientation to the four directions the "religion of natural monotheism" (*din al-hanifi*) is safeguarded.[7] Of course, the use of the term "*hanifi*" here refers very precisely to the example of Abraham, and this role of the Awtad may be compared to the Guardians of the Directions in Brahmanic doctrine, as well as a very similar understanding in the Chinese tradition.

The pilgrimage rites affirm in no uncertain terms the perpetuation of the traditions of Abraham by the religion of Islam. For example, the rite of "Stoning the Devil" reenacts the struggles of Abraham, and it might be worth considering here that the traditional markers erected to signify the positions of the Devil were stone pillars; however, such markers had – for they are no longer used - a practical purpose above all, and the proper name for these positions – *jamarat* – actually means "pebbles." There are, on the other hand, three sacred stones associated with Abraham that are visited on the Pilgrimage. The first is the Black Stone, built into the eastern corner of the Ancient House, that the Prophet Muhammad is reported to have kissed in greeting during his circumambulations. Another is the "Stone of Happiness," a vertical or standing stone believed to have been placed during the temple's original construction in the southern corner, and which the Prophet is also reported to have greeted. Concerning these stones the Messenger of God is

---

[6] Cf. Zechariah III, 9: "For behold the stone I have laid before Joshua; upon one stone shall be seven eyes…"
[7] Cf. Gilis, pages 51-3.

reported to have said, *"Touching them takes away sins."* The third is a stone set apart from the Ancient House, which served to support the prophet Abraham in his building work, and which bears the miraculous imprint of his foot. What is more, this stone, properly known as the "Station of Abraham," is specified in the second chapter of the Qur`an:

> *125. And when We made the House (at Mecca) a resort for mankind and sanctuary, (saying): Take as your place of worship the Station of Abraham. And We imposed a duty upon Abraham and Ishmael, (saying): Purify My House for those who go around and those who meditate therein and those who bow down and prostrate themselves (in worship).*

The location of the Ancient House, Mecca, is traditionally known as the "Navel of the Earth," recalling the literal meaning of omphalos. The Arabic word here for House, *bayt*, forms a proper name of the temple, *baytullah*, the House of God. The latter name is cognate with the word Bethel, the name bestowed by Jacob on the place of his pillar. The sacred stones of the pre-Islamic Arabs are called by the Greek form of the same word, betyls, signifying that these stones served as "houses" or supports for Divine influences among the descendants of Abraham. The word betyls was used in the Classical period more commonly for the venerated black stones or meteorites of the Roman East, such as the one belonging to the cult of Cybele that was relocated to Rome. Of course, a meteorite quite unmistakably embodies the link between what is above and below, and although a betyl need not necessarily be a meteorite, there is no question that meteorites have served quite naturally in this role.

The largest meteorite found in North America is known as the Willamette Meteorite, discovered near the confluence of two rivers in Oregon, due west from Mount Hood. Strangely, there was no impact crater in evidence. In modern times the meteorite was moved, sold, and samples were sliced from it, and it is now located at the American Museum of Natural history in New York City. Not surprisingly, the meteorite had long held special significance to Indians in the region, who were once numerous with a major cultural center nearby at Willamette Falls. Wrangling over ownership arose with the white American "discovery" and removal of the meteorite, and in 1903 two Indian witnesses testified in court that the extinct local tribe had "venerated the meteorite as their 'tomonowos' or visitor from the moon" or sky world, and that they "washed their faces in the water collected in the basins of the meteorite and that they put their arrows in the water before going to battle."[8] More recent legal wrangling over a hundred years later has failed to restore the meteorite to its original location, although Indians are now allowed to visit the "tomonowos" privately once a year.[9]

The traditional veneration of meteorites, or rather betyls, is remarkably widespread throughout North America. The following relates the traditional view of the Iron Creek Meteorite, now in the Royal Alberta Museum:

> Nanabozho, the Great Spirit or Manitou, placed the stone on a hill near the Battle River at Piwapiskoo, or Iron Creek, after the great flood. The elders said it had the power

---

[8] Erwin F. Lange, "The Willamette Meteorite: 1902-1962," West Linn Fair Board.

[9] On the surface, the relocation of the Willamette Meteorite may seem comparable to the Roman relocation of the black stone of Cybele; however, the latter example, with the betyl being installed in a new temple, partakes of Roman universality, whereas the American case deliberately violates the cultural identity of the "visitor," at the very least through its placement in a museum of "natural" history. For that matter, with Rome known as the "Red Apple" in Islamic civilization, the claim that New York City is the "Big Apple" seems an obvious parody.

> to protect the people of the Plains and the buffalo herds that sustained them...The stone existed to remind the Cree, the Nakoda (Stoneys) and the Blackfoot of the presence of manito, or spirit, in their lives. For generations it beckoned hunters, families and bands in a pilgrimage before and after the buffalo hunt.[10]

Warnings from medicine men that sickness, war, and the death of the buffalo would result from the stone's removal came to pass. The reason that the Reverend George McDougall decided to remove the meteorite "was likely due to the fact that he mistook the First Nations' veneration of the Manitou Stone for idolatry, something anathema to his religious beliefs. As such, he would have considered the sacrilege of its removal as something justified by his missionary purpose."[11] Of course, it would seem that such religious beliefs have abandoned their Abrahamic foundations. We have seen how these foundations were shared among traditional forms "adapted to new circumstances of time and place" following the Flood. It is especially important, therefore, to observe that traditional knowledge assigns the origin of the Iron Creek Meteorite to the period "after the great flood," and in the case of the Willamette Meteorite, the scientific explanation offered for the absence of a crater is displacement due to catastrophic floods. These examples may in turn be compared with the installation of the Black Stone in the Meccan temple that established the archetype of pilgrimage on earth.

---

[10] Quoted in Howard Plotkin, "The Iron Creek Meteorite: The Curious History of the Manitou Stone and the Claim for Its Repatriation," *Earth Sciences History*, volume 33, number 1, 2014, page 153.
[11] Ibid., page 158.

Other examples of North American meteorite betyls have been found. Not far from the Mexican border with the United States, an adobe citadel was constructed around the 1.5-ton meteorite at Casas Grandes, where it was discovered wrapped in linen like a human body. In Arizona, meteorites have been found in structures belonging to the ancient Sinagua people; one such complex in the Verde Valley was a shrine built upon a square plan, housing within its eastern wall a meteorite that had been wrapped in a cloth of feathers. Likewise in Arizona, the Navajo Meteorite, long held sacred by the Navajo Indians, had been found deliberately covered over by other rocks, in order to safeguard it.

Other sacred stones of traditional America, though not meteorites, may likewise be considered betyls, not least because their cupped appearance recalls so clearly the regmaglypts of meteorites. We have in mind especially the ovoid boulders known as "Rain Rocks" in Northern California, covered with cupules of various sizes, and associated with tribes such as the Karuk, who were named above because of their dedication to the guidance of the ancient white people. Now, the presence of cupules has been observed in places of extreme antiquity; for example, they appear on the uppermost surface of pillars at Göbekli Tepe.[12] Among the Achomawi Indians of California, cupules are said to be the footprints[13] of celestial beings and "the First People

---

[12] There are, in fact, even more remarkable connections to be made between this "oldest temple" and the ancient stones of America, yet the archaeologists seem incapable of considering them; these connections will hopefully be included in a future study.

[13] This identification of cupules with footprints recalls the Station of Abraham and the Divine command to worship there, as well as Lucy Thompson's claim that "our people still worship the hallowed places where once they trod." Footprints in stone must be acknowledged to be a mark of the Primordial Tradition; after all, in Sri Lanka, Adam's Peak is so called for the most ancient footprint upon its summit that is venerated by Muslims, Christians, Buddhists, and Brahmins alike (cf. Sperling, chapter 1).

who landed here *as the waters of the world flood receded.*"[14] For this reason, such boulders are known as "Jumping Rocks," recalling the cupule boulder in North Carolina known as Juaculla Rock where this jumping "Master-of-Game" is said to have landed. Further south in California, cupped boulders are called "Baby Rocks." In all these cases, petroglyphs of more recent origin appear alongside cupules, and it would seem that such marks are secondary, just as all these designations reflect the more particular concerns of those who venerate them; and so "Baby Rocks" may very well reflect the concerns of a dwindling population.

However, the celestial source of rain situates the "Rain Rocks" closest to the meteoric formulation of the betyl. The Rain Rock unearthed at Gottville[15] along the Klamath River is the best known, and the one figurative motif in evidence on its surface – bear prints – not only reinforces the association of cupules with footprints, but according to local lore it also indicates an astrological symbolism:

> According to the Old Ones, the Big Dipper controls the seasons. We call that constellation Great Bear in the Sky. Brilliant in the night, he lumbers to the left around the North Star...We stamp our circle dances in the same direction to keep the seasons in their proper order and to honor the Great Bear. Thousands of years ago we carved symbols into rock: the foot of a human and the foot of a bear...[16]

---

[14] Arlene Benson and Floyd Buckskin, "Achomawi Jumping Rocks and the Concept of the Test," *American Indian Rock Art*, volume XV, 1992, page 34. Italics added for emphasis.

[15] By a curious coincidence, the name of the white Americans' settlement has the meaning "Villa of God," and so approximates the very significance of "betyl."

[16] Thomas Doty, *Doty Meets Coyote*, Ashland: Blackstone, 2016, page 81. Here the movement of the stars corresponds to the polar

It is said that control over rain depended upon the application of water to the surface of the Rain Rock.[17] As we have seen with the Willamette Meteorite, the basins upon the surface have a function relating specifically to water, since to stop the rain these cupules would need to be filled with earth.[18] Indeed, this Rain Rock was unearthed during the construction of a modern roadway, and the Indians explained that it had been buried to prevent the recurrence of severe storms, since it had proven too powerful.[19] Much more likely, the stone had been unsuccessfully hidden, as was the case with the Navajo Meteorite. Despite such precautions, the Rain Rock was relocated to the museum at Fort Jones, a town named for a military fort of the Indian wars.

In his penetrating studies of Grail symbolism that so influenced John Michell, René Guénon focused on the enigmatic expression of Wolfram von Eschenbach for the Grail, *lapsit exillis*. Among its many meanings is "the stone fallen from the sky," and "precisely by reason of its origin, this stone is at it were 'in exile' in its terrestrial sojourn;" and a meteorite is doubtless also such a stone.[20] Beyond this, time and time again we have seen the betyls of America, meteoric or otherwise, removed from their traditional and providential placement due to the anti-traditional disruptions of white men. Any traditional world must provide a container for welcoming the descent of superior influences, like the Rain Rock itself. These influences descend at a geomantic center, upon an omphalos, and this center must be fixed, as we have

---

circumambulation of the pilgrims around the House of God in Mecca, in contradistinction from a clockwise solar turning.

[17] The control of rain through the manipulation of stone is widely recognized, and appears in a Celtic context in the legend of Yvain. Such rituals are still practiced in Islamic esoterism.

[18] This "deactivation" recalls the burial of sanctuaries such as Göbekli Tepe.

[19] This information is provided by the Fort Jones Museum.

[20] "Lapsit exillis" in *Symbols of Sacred Science*.

seen, to serve as the goal of the pilgrim.[21] Sadly, so many sacred stones have been exiled from their very purpose in America, and it is no wonder if the landscape of such a world should become a wasteland.

---

[21] Of course, the Stone of Destiny is a special case, since it accompanies the High Kings. Even so, cyclical conditions may require displacement, such as was the case with Abu Qubays and the Black Stone.

The American West
Detail from a 1776 map incorporating European and Chinese mythic elements

7

Between East and West

In "The Omphalos and the Sacred Stones" from *The King of the World*, René Guénon draws attention to a Chinese legend that he compares to the Celtic "Island of the Four Masters." This legend appears in a Taoist source, and concerns a visit to four masters on a distant island inhabited by *chen jen* ("True Men"), "those who have been restored to their 'primordial state.'"[1] Guénon ends the chapter indicating the centrality of the number five, and that "analogous traditions are also to be found in Central America."[2] Now, even secular scholarship has not failed to admit the many clear similarities connecting Chinese civilization and the Olmec culture especially. An attempt by a member of the Smithsonian Institution to address these connections appeared in 1975, entitled "The Transpacific Origin of Mesoamerican Civilization: A Preliminary Review of the Evidence and its Theoretical Implications."[3] However, the notion that the Chinese had been present in America long

---

[1] Elsewhere Guénon equates this True Man with *El-Insânul-qadîm* or "Primordial Man" of Islamic esoterism, a rank below that of *El-Insânul-Kâmil*; he associates the difference between these ranks as comparable to that between "virtual immortality and actually realized immortality" (1975, page 124). While *qadim* in Arabic signifies "primordial" or "ancient," the closely related word *qadam* means "foot;" and this recalls the footprints of the ancients described in the last chapter. Curiously, these words share the same root elements as the names "Madoc" and "Modoc."

[2] Op. cit., page 60-1.

[3] Published in the *American Anthropologist*.

before the Europeans was by no means new, since 18th century European scholarship had identified America as the mythical land of Fusang, based on distances reported in ancient Chinese accounts; and so mapmakers at the time depicted Fusang on the American West Coast. This identification has fallen out of favor, despite a lack of convincing evidence to the contrary.[4]

In 2003, a sinkhole revealed another "sign of the times" to archaeologists working at the ruined city called Teotihuacan in Mexico. This city was once known as Tollan, a name comparable to Tula; and even though it is not considered among the works of the Olmecs, it shares characteristics with them. For their part, the Aztecs who had come to inhabit the city after it had lain in ruins for nearly a thousand years considered it the work of the giants of a previous age. The sinkhole opened onto a tunnel running beneath the so-called Pyramid of the Feathered Serpent, and by now the extent of the accidental discovery has become clear, if not its interpretation. What had remained hidden even to the Aztecs was a subterranean world in miniature, in which pools of mercury represented bodies of water within a mountainous landscape, and mineral powders within the walls and ceilings glittered like stars. Directly under the artificial mountain of the pyramid, four statues of greenstone had been placed, and in chambers to the north and south, hundreds of metallized spheres of various dimensions.

All this presents an impenetrable mystery to those incapable of suspecting the influence of Chinese esoterism. For what concerns us here, it is perhaps sufficient to provide a comparison with the pyramid mausoleum of the First Emperor of China, whose preoccupation with finding the

---

[4] Unhelpful in this regard are the recent claims of the project entitled *1421: The Year China Discovered America*, in which ample evidence of an ancient Chinese presence - along with erroneous interpretations of monuments such as the Elizabethan Newport Tower – has been taken out of proper context to support an unsubstantiated Ming-era visit.

Elixir of Life has been well established: "Mercury was used to fashion imitations of the hundred rivers, the Yellow River and the Yangtze, and the seas, constructed in such a way that they seemed to flow. Above were representations of the heavenly bodies, below, the features of the earth."[5]

The building of this mausoleum is more or less contemporary with the foundations of Teotihuacan, and so predates the construction of the Pyramid of the Feathered Serpent. We need not be concerned if the latter pyramid is not a mausoleum, since what is essential in these examples is the symbolism of the sacred mountain and the "Grotto-Heaven," to use the Taoist expression, concealed beneath it. The Grotto-Heavens "do not suffer from floods, wars, epidemics, illnesses, old age or death,"[6] and so correspond to the Elixir of Life.

Similarly, the location of Fusang is associated with Taoist immortality. According to Chinese cosmology, immortals lived on three "spirit mountains" or islands in the far eastern seas, and upon Mount Penglai in particular all things appeared white.[7] Above all, however, this sacred geography of the eastern seas was associated with a land called Fusang, after a cosmic tree that bore the sun upon its branches. According to his official historian, the First Emperor sought the sacred herbs believed to grow in these lands. The court wizard Xu Fu undertook a quest for the immortal Anqi Sheng on Mount Penglai in 219 B.C., but a monstrous fish blocked his expedition. The attempt was renewed in 210 with the addition of archers to join the pure youths and various craftsmen who had been selected for the

---

[5] Sima Qian, *Records of the Grand Historian*, translated by Burton Watson, Hong Kong: Columbia University Press, 1993, page 63.

[6] "Grotto-Heavens and Blissful Lands," in *The Encyclopedia of Taoism*, New York: Routledge, 2009, pages 368.

[7] Here we find again the "white mountain" presented as a spiritual center. As far as the geography of islands is concerned, it is worth acknowledging that early maps of the Americas depict California as an island, and this detail was perpetuated with notable persistence.

quest. None of the ships under Xu Fu's command ever returned to China, giving rise to subsequent speculation, such as the implausible notion that the search was satisfied upon reaching Japan.

In 1875, the publication of *Fusang: The Discovery of America by Chinese Buddhist Monks in the Fifth Century* by Charles Godfrey Leland renewed the identification of Fusang with western America. At the same time in California itself, the first comprehensive effort to report on its last indigenous people was being prepared. This was the work of Stephen Powers, who turned his attention to his subject after traveling across America from North Carolina on foot. Powers presented his reports piece by piece on particular tribes, but his work was so valuable that he eventually received an offer to have it published in one volume by a government office. There were two stipulations, however, to which Powers agreed: the estimate of California's population before European contact would be drastically reduced from his original figure by at least more than half; and his conviction that the "pre-aboriginal" people from whom the Indians of California descended were Chinese would not be mentioned.[8] Even though Powers had already defended this latter position in academic circles, its omission from *Tribes of California* could only frustrate inquiries into traditional connections between Fusang and California.

Nevertheless, such connections exist. For example, Powers mentions in his discussion of the Shasta Indians a legend in passing, the importance of which has hitherto been unrecognized: "Originally, the sun had nine brothers, alike to himself, flaming hot with fire, so that the world was like to

---

[8] See Robert F. Heizer's introduction to the 1976 reprint of *Tribes of California* (op. cit.). Alfred Kroeber called his predecessor's work "one of the most remarkable documents ever printed by any government."

perish; but the coyote slew nine of the brothers, and so saved mankind from burning up."[9]

Here, beyond a doubt, is an echo of the very ancient Chinese legend of Yi the Archer,[10] who shoots down nine suns with his arrows after they had become infected by demonic birds. Now, neither archery nor birds are specifically mentioned in this very brief summary of the Shasta legend, even though the shooting of arrows against demonic birds is in fact a widespread motif in traditional America. However, what makes this reference to nine suns so significant is that the legend of Yi the Archer is set specifically in the land of Fusang. Indeed, the name "Fusang" derives from the cosmic tree found there, upon which the birds that carry the suns come to rest.[11]

Based upon his personal experiences of language and custom, Powers suggested that the Chinese influence on the tribes of California was limited to regions south of Mount Shasta. This should be revised, given the occurrence of this legend of Fusang among a people living north of the mountain. [12] Relatable to this is a very distinctive characteristic of tribes in Northern California, discernable in his reports, that in fact extends at least as far north as the

---

[9] Op. cit., page 251. The legend continues with an account of Coyote's slaying of nine moons.

[10] Yi is associated with the Elixir of Life through his wife, who inhabits the sphere of the moon along with the rabbit that prepares the elixir according to Chinese cosmology. In this connection, it is worth observing that the Aztecs as well as the Cree share the image of the "Moon Rabbit."

[11] The shooting of the nine suns is made necessary by the birds' alighting all at once, and so failing to carry the suns in sequence. More importantly, the shooting of the nine to leave one is an expression of a return to the center, since the circle surrounding its center is customarily divided by factors of nine. Just as five corresponds to the central position in relation to the quaternary, so does its multiple ten in relation to the circle of nine.

[12] Indeed, European maps that indicate Fusang on the American west coast prefer a region more to the north.

Columbia River, where his attention did not reach. This characteristic is a focus, unique to American Indian tradition, on the importance of the number five, as well as its multiple ten, as we have even seen in the legend of the sun and his nine brothers. The importance of five in Chinese civilization is too obvious to insist upon, and so the correspondence is clear. There is even a very particular way in which the number five relates to the land of Fusang in Chinese sources: as indicated in the title of Leland's book, there is a detailed report of a Buddhist mission from Central Asia reaching Fusang, and the number of missionaries was precisely five.

If only by virtue of his being the earliest of authorities, we should not disregard Powers' learned opinion on the influence of the ancient Chinese in California; after all, the First Emperor's expedition may account for the evidence that Powers could not ignore.[13] In any case, given the context of our investigations into traditional forms, we should not overlook those of the Chinese court, and in particular the authority of the wizard sent on the Emperor's quest. To begin with, we should recognize the unmistakably alchemical context of the quest, since it pertained to the Elixir of Life, reminding us of the relationship between Hermeticism and Idris and so with the Primordial Tradition. The Chinese title of a court magician was *wu*, from the Old Chinese *$^*m^yag$*; but according to Victor Mair, *$^*m^yag$* is actually a loan word from

---

[13] Certainly the giant redwood trees of California, unmatched anywhere else on earth, recall the eponymous solar tree of Fusang. Given the specific inclusion of archers and craftsmen on the expedition of Xu Fu, it is also worth mentioning that the bows of California are strikingly similar to the traditional Chinese form, being recurved and composite in construction and drawn with the use of the thumb; in Islamic civilization, the prophet Abraham is considered the originator of the craft of composite bow construction. It would also be worthwhile to compare the stone structures called *tsektsel* by the Yurok with the principles of Chinese geomancy, displayed most concretely in the horseshoe-shaped "Turtleback Tombs."

the Old Persian *magus*, meaning "specialist in ritual." These Magi "professed knowledge of astronomy, astrology, and medicine, of how to control the winds and weather by potent magic, and of how to contact the spirit world,"[14] and the same was true of the *wu* of the Chinese court.

We may recall that between the Celts and the Brahmins, Clement of Alexandria describes "the Magi among the Persians who announced beforehand the birth of the Saviour, being led by a star till they arrived in the land of Judea," whose tradition should therefore also be included among those forms that arose through the fusion of the Atlantean and Hyperborean currents. Concerning their origin, John Bennett makes the following observation in his study of the "Masters of Wisdom" of Islamic esoterism: "The Magi were members of a caste or class that existed in Central Asia from before the time of Zoroaster."[15] As far as their successors are concerned, it may be offered that a distinctive characteristic of the Magi was the insistence upon wearing white.[16] The Biblical mention of the Magi provides a clear example within the Abrahamic scriptures of those who watch the heavens in the service of monotheism. For René Guénon, the Magi of the Gospels represent nothing less than the Primordial Tradition.[17]

---

[14] Elizabeth Wayland Barber, *The Mummies of Ürümchi*, New York: Norton and Company, 1999, page 201. If a possible transmission through China of a tradition belonging to the "barbarians" seems unlikely, this is precisely the case with the more recent rise of Buddhism, of Indian origin, in China.

[15] *The Masters of Wisdom*, Santa Fe: Bennett Books, 1995, page 51.

[16] For example, Bennett describes the first teacher of the Master of Wisdom Ahmad Yasawi as the "alchemist and magician Baba Arslan" (ibid., page 97), who was believed to be a companion of the Prophet Muhammad half a millennium before; he is now thought to have been a leader of the Mubayyidiyya, the "wearers of white," who patterned themselves upon earlier Magi.

[17] Cf. *The King of the World*, chapter 4.

In relation to Indian America, the meaning of *magus* as a "specialist in ritual" may be compared with Kroeber's characterization of the medicine men of Northern California as "formalists;" and we have already had occasion to mention in this context astronomy, as well as an example of "weather control." Above all else, however, we need to recognize that the Yurok word for medicine man, or "white doctor," is *meges*. In this connection, it may be observed that in her treatment of the ancient white people, Lucy Thompson prefers the spelling "Wa-gas" over the more phonetically correct "Wogey;" and this seems very curious, given that the Yurok name for a Chinese person is *"we'ges."*

In recognizing an ancient Eastern presence in western America, we are reminded of the position of America as a place "in-between." Of course, East and West naturally meet in the "Middle" East; but America is rather discomfitingly at the antipodes of the lands holy to the Abrahamic faiths. In a similar manner, Dante imagined his mountain of Purgatory at the antipodes of Jerusalem, and Purgatory stands between the Fire and Paradise. America in turn stands between the memory of the fall of Atlantis and the sacred geography of Fusang, a Land of the Sun. In his imagining of Purgatory, Dante took inspiration from what is known in Islamic theology as the *barzakh*, the state of the dead between this world and the Day of Judgment. Yet barzakh signifies also a barrier that separates as well as mediates, and so has been compared to a lens functioning as a point of inversion; a barzakh is therefore "the starting point of a separate perspective."[18] Indeed America is a place where perspective is reversed, since the Orient is seen to the west and the Occident to the east. Given this observation, it may even be said that there are two Easts and two Wests on earth, as seen from the Middle East and from its antipodes.

---

[18] Titus Burckhardt, "Concerning the 'Barzakh,'" *Mirror of the Intellect*, Albany: SUNY Press, 1987, page 194.

Remarkably, the expression "*Lord of the Two Easts and Lord of the Two Wests*" appears in the revelation of the Qur'an.[19]

For traditional America, furthest west was the Land of the Dead; it is for this reason, even though Powers did not insist upon it, that the Konkow Maidu perceived the Chinese recently arrived in California from the west to be "dead Indians come back to life."[20] By the end of the 19th century, millenarian movements had enchanted both the American West and the Chinese East, in hopes of bringing the tyranny of Christian invaders to an end. Whereas the Ghost Dances were essentially peaceful and the Boxer Rebellion was militant, they shared a conviction that the spirits of the dead would return to assist the living in the restoration of vanishing traditions. In a sense, then, these movements also searched for an Elixir of Life.

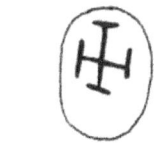

Old Chinese **m^yag*

---

[19] LV: 17.
[20] Stephen Powers, "Aborigines of California: An Indo-Chinese Study," *Atlantic Monthly* 33, 1874, page 313.

Cross pattée

8

Treasures of Red and White

Among all the peoples of traditional America, the Hopi are recognized especially for the accuracy of their prophecies anticipating various corruptions of the modern period. These visions concern the fourth in a series of worlds according to Hopi cosmology; the Third World was destroyed, significantly enough, by a flood. A Fifth World is expected to follow the present one, and its arrival is associated above all with a figure known as Pahana or Bahana. Now, just like the Yurok Wo'gey, "Bahana" means simply "white man," and the traditions of the two tribes concerning ancient white people may further be seen to converge on the subject of his return. The Hopi consider the origin of Bahana to be identical with their own, and is traditionally expressed in geomantic terms as the *sipapu*, a point of emergence from a subterranean origin.[1] Just as the Hopi history of the present world following the flood proceeds from an origin shared with Bahana, this world may alternatively be understood in spatial terms to proceed outwardly from a central point. At this sipapu, a tablet was broken on the occasion of the parting of the Hopi from their "white brother" Bahana, with the latter keeping a piece of the tablet, by which he would be recognized when he is reunited with the Hopi. As in Yurok tradition, the return of the white person announces the arrival of a world renewed, yet it is

---

[1] Of course, this may be compared with the various sites dedicated to the veneration of the Companions of the Cave. The Hopi sipapu is usually located in the Grand Canyon.

foretold in the case of Bahana that he will be distinctively wearing red.

It has already been established that the "white" characteristic of the ancient white people refers above all to their sacerdotal authority, with red being the complementary attribute of the warrior. With this mind, the description of Bahana as wearing red would seem to indicate a union of these attributes. However, for the Hopi - whose very name indicates their preference for peace - it was the capacity for violence demonstrated by arriving Europeans that seems to have excluded Christians from being identified with Bahana: "First were the Catholics, but they were thrown out - unfortunately not without some sad events, such as the massacre and destruction at Awatovi. Then there were Mennonites, Mormons, Jehovah's Witnesses, Seventh Day Adventists, and Baptists...The missionaries came telling the Hopis and the Tewas that the old traditional ways were barbaric..." [2] How, then, are we to understand this conjunction of white and red?

It is most helpful in this regard to consider the doctrines of Hermeticism. The colors of white and red are integral to understanding the alchemical process, and correspond, in fact, with the *gunas* of Hindu doctrine. According to the latter, white is the color associated with an upward tendency, in keeping with sacerdotal guidance, whereas red indicates an expansive tendency involving action in the world, and especially the duties of the warrior caste. Yet somewhat paradoxically, the stage called "whitening" must precede that of "reddening" in the alchemical work; but this is precisely because the goal of the work is an embodiment of the spirit *in the world*. [3]

---

[2] *Hopi Voices: Recollections, Traditions, and Narratives of the Hopi Indians*, edited by Harold Courlander, Albuquerque: University of New Mexico Press, 1982, page 142.

[3] *Cf.* Titus Burckhardt, *Alchemy: Science of the Cosmos, Science of the Soul*, Shaftesbury: Element Books, 1986, pages 182-3.

Significantly enough, the emblem of "whitening" is the moon, whereas that of "reddening" is the sun.

The so-called Age of Exploration for Christian Europeans was not an expression of an "upward tendency." It is no coincidence that 1492 marks both the opening of the Americas as well as the final expulsion of the other Abrahamic communities from Christian Spain.[4] The word "conquest" marks both developments, since the former came to be led by the Conquistadores, while the latter was called the Reconquista rather inaccurately, since it was not a "reconquest" at all. Both are expressions of an expansive tendency, altogether "red," and yet both operated under a residual emblem of the Crusades that was characteristically red and white.

This symbol of the "cross pattée"[5] properly belonged to the Order of the Temple of Solomon, or Templars, a monastic order of knights originally created to rival the chivalry of Islam in defense of Christian pilgrims to Jerusalem. Significantly, their headquarters had been the Dome of the Rock, the betyl of Jerusalem,[6] and during their presence there had served as a bridge between Christendom and Islam.[7] The failure of the Kingdom of Jerusalem,

---

[4] This may be compared to the modern state of Israel and the Jews' persecution of communities likewise belonging to the "family of Abraham."

[5] Very curiously, this cross – the name of which literally means "footed" - is essentially identical to the "cross potent" that stood for "magus" in Old Persian. Obviously, neither should be confused with the Christian crucifix. The balanced structure of these crosses invites comparisons to the cosmic Awtad; with this in mind, it is interesting to observe that for Christendom, the "Redcrosse Knight" is Saint George, who is called by the Muslims al-Khidr.

[6] This betyl – called Rock or Foundation Stone - bears the venerated footprint of the Prophet Muhammad, since here is believed to be the location of the angelic Ladder (mi`raj) of his Night Journey and Ascension.

[7] See Ponsoye, especially chapter VI.

followed by the dissolution of the Templars, brought an end to the possibility of an armed vocation guided by monastic vows; so too was their red and white emblem deprived of its true significance.[8] Nevertheless, there is a strange popular fascination with the notion that the extinct Templars somehow contributed to the "secret history" of America, and this fascination is focused very specifically on a supposed "treasure of the Templars." This fascination is akin to the search for the descendants of Prince Madoc,[9] since both concern a missing reconciliation of the red and the white, albeit formulated in different ways.

There is, however, a much more tangible manner in which America's foundation was oriented to the Temple of Solomon, and this is through the doctrines of Freemasonry. Masonry, of course, traces its origin to the building of Solomon's Temple, and so is a craft initiation related to the Abrahamic tradition; in fact, as René Guénon has indicated: "if we wish to go beyond Solomon, we could with far more reason go back further still to Abraham himself,"[10] who, as we have seen, was the builder of the temple in Mecca.[11] As a

---

[8] Still, Christian Hermeticism preserved at least an awareness of the alchemical work. The Brotherhood of the Rosy Cross in particular succeeded the Templars as the bridge between Christendom and the lands of Islam; the emphasis of the brotherhood, however, was on healing, more in keeping with the example of Jesus, and also recalling the focus of the Chinese alchemists. The initial efforts of John Winthrop, Jr., should be mentioned in this regard, since his contribution to New England culture was indebted to the vision of Dr. John Dee. Cf. Walter W. Woodward, *Prospero's America*, Chapel Hill: University of North Carolina Press, 2010.

[9] See chapter 1.

[10] *Studies in Freemasonry and the Compagnonnage*, Hillsdale: Sophia Perennis, 2004, page 231. Craft initiations in the world of Islam were traditionally governed by the ideals of "spiritual chivalry" (*futuwwah*), and these ideals were likewise traced to Abraham. Cf. *The Royal Book of Spiritual Chivalry*, Chicago: Kazi Publications, 1999.

[11] It is of interest in this connection to note that the Ancient Arabic Order of the Nobles of the Mystic Shrine or "Shriners," an American

craft initiation, Masonry clearly belongs to a domain of action, at least in its original "operative" form;[12] and so its necessary allegiance to the monotheism of Abraham is expressed by its dedication to work for "the glory of the Great Architect of the Universe." Nevertheless, for Guénon, whose writings on Masonic symbolism comprise a significant part of his work, a distinction should be made between the Masonic orthodoxy of George Washington, for example, and those elements transmitted by Benjamin Franklin, who he called "the agent of certain extremely suspect influences."[13] Given the lack of sacerdotal authority in the founding of America, this scenario should not be too surprising; but it is important to recognize here a nimrodian potential. Similarly, the American pretense of separating "church and state" enables the latter to become nimrodian,[14] and no manner of

---

fraternity for master Masons, is named for the shrine or temple in Mecca.

[12] Albert Mackey in his *Encyclopaedia of Freemasonry and its Kindred Sciences* cites *"banah"* as the Hebrew word "to build," and Guénon (ibid., page 207) mentions its Arabic equivalent. The similarity to the name Bahana is interesting, at least, especially since a hallmark of the ancient white people was the building of stone monuments.

[13] Cf. the French edition of *Étude sur la Franc-Maçonnerie et le Compagnonnage*. Such elements are on display on the reverse of America's Great Seal.

[14] Of course, the original cause of this "obsession" was simple defiance of the Church of England's exclusivity. For his part, HRH the Prince of Wales famously challenged this exclusivity by declaring his intention to defend "faith itself which is so often under threat in our day." With the prince, to whom John Michell once dedicated (with permission) his work, we are most fortunate to expect a "philosopher king" in keeping with Plato's ideal. Not only does his full name include George, recalling England's patron saint, but he is also, like his heirs, named Arthur.

"checks and balances" may substitute for the balance bestowed by spiritual influences.[15]

Even though their racial identity gave them the appearance of being white, the new Americans did not display the peacefulness that characterized the ancient white people, and that in a general sense is symbolized by white. We have seen that the Yuroks were originally deceived by appearances, but before long were able to separate the "foreigners" from their expectations of the white people's return. In relation to the Hopi expectation of the Bahana wearing red, the new Americans may rather be said to have been "red" or worldly people wearing "white," with white here indicating the superficial residues of a vanished medieval Christendom. Moreover, these residues may have actually served to excuse the means employed by America to accomplish its "Manifest Destiny." If it is suggested that the monks of the Spanish missions in America maintained at least a sacerdotal integrity, we should not forget that it was placed in the service of worldly expansion, and so participated in an inversion of the proper relationship between the spiritual and temporal. Indeed, efforts to Christianize the Indians generally demanded rather the extinction of "barbaric" tradition in favor of behaviors adhering to the expectations of the state, rather than sacerdotal integrity.[16]

A proper relationship of the spiritual and temporal is an ideal inherent to the Abrahamic tradition of Islam. An early Christian witness described the knights of Islam as

---

[15] After all, the name that we have observed identifying a spiritual center, Tula, means "balance" in Sanskrit. Curiously, the very similar Tülay in Turkish means "moon."

[16] Even though the new Americans did not fulfill the Hopi expectation, it is nevertheless remarkable to observe the Christian names borne by representatives of Indian tradition, such as with Chief "Joseph," since such names very well belong to the nation of Abraham. There are also Joshua Indians along the Oregon coast, and so it is worth noting that Joshua is known in Islam as the son of Nūn.

"cavaliers in the day and monks in the night;" and just as the day traditionally follows the night that precedes it, their efforts on the field of struggle traditionally depended upon a spiritual orientation. This is well indicated by the teaching of the Prophet of Islam concerning the struggles of the battlefield being lesser than the spiritual "greater jihad." Given the relevance of red and white in this context, we must consider above all a Tradition (*hadith*) included in a collection of unquestionable authenticity (*sahih*), under the chapter heading: "This human family (*ummah*) would be destroyed by killing one another." Leaving aside the tragic description, we draw attention in particular to its beginning:

> *Thawban reported that the Messenger of Allah (may peace be upon him) said: Allah contracted the earth for me, I was shown its Easts and its Wests; and He bestowed upon me two treasures, the red and the white.*[17]

As we have also seen indicated by the title "Melchizedek," the Divine Messenger Muhammad demonstrated a balance of spiritual authority and temporal power, with the former preceding the latter in his sacred biography; and chivalric and spiritual initiatory benefits may indeed be signified by the red and the white treasures. No doubt this balance may be pertinent to mention before describing the violence that results from its absence. What is more, since this Tradition belongs to an apocalyptic context, it is essential to consider the references in Islamic esoterism to a hidden prophetic inheritance known as *jafr*, sometimes divided into red and white formulations, that is made known at the end of the world. Yet here again the same significance appears, since its red form pertains to sacred armor and weapons, whereas the white contains spiritual secrets of the Abrahamic traditions,

---

[17] Sahih Muslim.

especially concerning apocalyptic events.[18] Sometimes the Jafr is expressed more completely by the phrase *Kitab al-jafri wal-jami`a*, indicating a book that contains the secrets of destiny properly belonging to Heavenly Tablets. Even more remarkably, the indication of another East and West suggests America itself, as we have seen, especially in the context of "killing one another" that has been and still is facilitated by the use of firearms.

Among the Yuroks and those tribes remembering the traditions of the ancient white people, the treasures of their World-Renewal Ceremonies to balance the earth include the white deerskin, ornamented with the red feathers of the woodpecker, as well as great blades of obsidian.[19] The situating of treasures of "the red and the white" in the context of the apocalypse even more explicitly evokes the expected return of the Bahana, since he bears part of a treasure that was long ago divided between red and white peoples. It is of interest to note that the part belonging to Bahana is identified by the head of a figure depicted upon it,[20] and so a comparison may be made with the two forms of the letter Nūn, an upper and a lower, that when brought

---

[18] The Jafr is an especially Muhammadan treasure, inherited through his Noble Family, yet its contents are traced to various prophets of the past; this treasure may therefore be understood to confirm the rank of Muhammad as the "Seal of Prophets." According to the doctrines of *futuwwah*, prophecy originated with Adam and is sealed by Muhammad, and Abraham is considered its pole.

[19] Perhaps it is not without significance that the immortals of Taoism, such as Anqi Sheng who was sought on Mount Penglai, are associated with the white deer, as well as the crane, symbol of immortality, whose white feathers crowned by a red crest was seen to embody the proper balance of yin and yang. A symbol of Hyperborean origin, the white deer is likewise present in the Celtic tradition.

[20] Cf. Harold Courlander, *The Fourth World of the Hopis: The Epic Story of the Hopi Indians as Preserved in their Legends and Traditions*, Albuquerque: University of New Mexico Press, 1987, page 31.

together become the sign of the sun – as well as of gold - in Hermeticism:[21]

We have already seen that America has been identified with a mythical Land of the Sun. In the legend of Fusang, however, the solar birds and the suns borne by them are subject to corruption; yet this is in keeping with the laws of symbolism: "it is also true that the symbolism of the sun presents in itself the two opposing aspects, life-giving and death-dealing, productive and destructive, as we have already noted in connection with weapons that represent the `solar ray.'"[22] Of course, the life-preserving arrows of Yi the Archer must be included among the weapons representing the "solar ray," and so both solar attributes are present in the legend of Fusang. Remarkably, the Great Seal of America, or more exactly its coat of arms, displays both a solar bird – the eagle – and arrows of war in its talon; in the context of Fusang, however, can we be certain that the bird of the Great Seal is not predominantly "death-dealing?"

---

[21] According to Islamic esoterism, the Nūn corresponds to the celestial sphere of the sun, and has the numerical value of fifty. When its two forms are united, the letter may be seen to have doubled, and so becomes equivalent to one hundred. Since fifty and one hundred are simply elaborations of five and ten, we return here to the symbolism of the latter numbers, with centrality clearly indicated by the point of the Nūn.
[22] *Symbols of Sacred Science*, page 186.

American Coat of Arms
Indian Peace Medal of 1792

9

The Western Phoenix

In the landscape of the apocalypse according to Islam, the presence of the "western sun" is of central importance. Specifically, the "sun rising from the place of its setting" is counted among the five principal signs of the End of Time. It appears also in the title of the most valuable book of Islamic esoterism pertaining explicitly to the apocalypse, the `Anqa' mughrib fi ma`rifat khatm al-awliya' wa shams al-maghrib ("The Wondrous Anqa in the Knowledge of the Seal of Sainthood and the Sun of the West") by the "Greatest Master" Ibn `Arabi. Here the western sun signifies the expected inheritor of the Prophet Muhammad who gathers the faithful in preparation for the descent of Jesus. This inheritor is named al-Mahdi and called the Caliph of God, and is the one expected to reveal and explain the contents of the Jafr; this is indeed a speciality very comparable to what is expected of the Bahana, the ability to explain what is revealed on the restored tablet. The Jafr properly belongs to what is known in Islamic esoterism as the Science of Letters (`ilm ul-hurūf) – to which the symbolism of the Nūn belongs - and is associated with a spiritual rank designated by the alchemical term, the "Red Sulphur." Given this alchemical terminology in the context of spirituality, it is clear that this solar "reddening" corresponds exactly with the wearing of red by the white Bahana.

Concerning al-Mahdi, the Greatest Master explains:

> *He will wipe out injustice and its people and uphold Religion (al-Din), and he will breathe the spirit back*

> *into Islam. He will reinvigorate Islam after its degradation and bring it back to life after its death...*
>
> *He will manifest Religion as it (really) is in Itself, the Religion by which the Messenger of God would judge and rule if he were there. He will eliminate the different schools (of religious law) so that only the Pure Religion (Qur'an 39:3) remains, and his enemies will be those who blindly follow the scholars of the law...*[1]

Since there are four main schools of religious law in Islam, this reference to eliminating the four by returning to their source recalls the central significance of five.[2] This symbolism may therefore be compared to the Fifth World inaugurated by Bahana.

Now, the presence of the name "Anqa" in the title of this work is strange. The Anqa of Arab lore is imagined as a giant bird, sometimes with human features. According to a tradition recounted by the historian Mas`udi, the Anqa had been created at the beginning of time wondrous, and was known in the Temple of Solomon; after finding a new habitat in Arabia, it fell into tyranny, even feeding on children, and so was exterminated there by Divine permission.[3] The form of this Anqa may easily be compared with hybrid forms in American Indian legend, such as the Birdman of the Mound

---

[1] James W. Morris, "The End of Time," in Ibn al 'Arabi, op. cit., page 69.

[2] This apocalyptic restoration has in fact already been parodied by the Wahhabis, because their "Salafi" posturing has invented a fundamentalist school to challenge the validity of the orthodox four schools. Of course, their counter-traditional agenda reached its fullest development with I.S.I.S.' declaration of a false caliphate in 2014.

[3] Since the name "Anqa" is closely related through its root to the Hebrew name "Anakim," it is significant that the Anakim were considered descendants of the fallen Nephilim.

Builders or the Hopi Man-eagle, as well as the ubiquitous Thunderbird; and there is even a linguistic similarity between the Anqa and the giant Ang bird of Lake Tahoe. A most ancient form of this demonic storm bird may be discovered in Mesopotamia, where the Anzû is guilty of stealing the sacred Tablet of Destinies, a treasure that may be easily compared with the Jafr. What is more, there is in these comparisons consistent evidence of a duality of aspects, originally wondrous, then tyrannical – or rather nimrodian - that also recalls the solar birds of Fusang. Among the Navajo, the mountain called by white Americans Ship Rock is known as Winged Rock, since it is remembered for having kindly brought the Navajo through the air to their present homeland; yet this location is at the same time remembered for having been the home of man-eating birds.

In the title of the book by Shaykh Muhyiddin Ibn `Arabi, Anqa is qualified by the word *mughrib*, meaning "strange" or "wondrous," and it is obviously related here to the word for west, *maghrib*, the place of the sunset.[4] As a wondrous bird of the sun, the Anqa becomes identical to the phoenix in the language of Hermeticism,[5] a symbol of cyclic renewal that is especially relevant in the apocalyptic setting of a western sunrise. This title declares a renewal of the wondrous Anqa from extinction, reborn in its original form, akin to the revivification of religion by al-Mahdi.[6]

---

[4] Among the four directions, the Thunderbird is most consistently associated with the West.

[5] The word "phoenix" refers to red, and we have already noted the Yurok formulation of the "red eagle." Given that the phoenix is most often renewed by fire, it is also interesting to note that the Hopi fragment of the tablet of Bahana is said to be in the possession of the Fire Clan.

[6] Such a renewal may be compared to the awakening of the Companions of the Cave, especially since Islamic esotericism recognizes a correspondence between the Companions and the seven chief ministers of al-Mahdi.

We have seen that among the duties of the saintly Awtad is the safeguarding of the "religion of natural monotheism," that is, those sacerdotal doctrines and methods followed by the *hanif*. Among the so-called Abrahamic traditions, Islam honors foremost the "rule" or "nation of Abraham:"

> 135. *And they say: be Jews or Christians, then ye will be rightly guided. Say (unto them, O Muhammad): Nay, but (we belong to) the nation of Abraham, the hanif, and he was not of the idolaters.*[7]

As we have suggested, the traditional worlds under Abraham's spiritual authority are legion, and should in fact include all those "naturally inclined to monotheism." It is precisely because of Abraham the father[8] that the Hopi and the Bahana are "brothers."

Given the accord between traditional America and the "religion of natural monotheism," explanations to account for an ancient Abrahamic influence have in fact been offered. Most notably, a chief of the Cherokee, Charles R. Hicks, suggested the following in the context of the sacerdotal role of the Aní-Kutánî:

> ...'tis not (im)emprobable to suppose but that this class of men had officiated as in their sacrifices at such times as was set apart for that purpose, as it hase (has) been represented to have been the ancient custom observed among our ancestors; and perhaps,

---

[7] Surah II.

[8] The use of "father" here may be insufficient, given the "maternal" spirituality of Abraham according to Islamic esoterism. Cf. Charles-André Gilis, *Marie en Islam*, Paris: Études Traditionnelles, 1990, chapter VIII.

> too, they may have been teachers in detached parts in the mosaical law, which is still found some traces of it among the present race, as in the handling of dead persons, and the monthly times with women, and the only difference of what is in holy writ & the tradition, is the nights instead of days, and the evening bath & the other the morning, beside others recorded in the bible, from which there is some grounds to suppose our ancestors may have (been) neighbors to the children of Israel, and by their intercourse with them may have obtained the knowledge what is recited above; and like (a) great deal more, which may be forgotten after they were stripped of their offices; and it is also not unlikely that after their office were disannul by the nation, they might have shifted their profession to that of the Jugglers and Doctors, for it is found in our days that the Jugglers & doctors possess more knowledge of the Traditions of this nation than any others among the present race.[9]

Here we are very close indeed to recognizing the identity of the White People, even if their Abrahamic affiliation is more ancient and less "mosaical" than the chief presumes. Another explanation from the California missions is somewhat more challenging, though clearly in keeping with the symbolism being considered:

> In 1773 a Salinan Indian woman (believed to be a centenarian) related to the San Antonio Mission padres that her grandfather told her stories about a man who visited their land

---

[9] Letter to Chief John Ross, 1 March 1826.

> upon four different occasions – each time arriving on the wings of a large bird. His clothes and teachings were identical to those of the mission San Antonio padres.[10]

The "large bird" of this report no doubt recalls the Anqa in its wondrous form, created "at the beginning of time."[11]

We have seen that the medicine men of California healed in accordance with the sacerdotal guidance of the ancient white people who are also the "First People," and were believed to restore the world to its "original condition." The original human condition, of course, belongs to Adam in the Abrahamic traditions. In Islam, he is recognized as the first Caliph of God, the Primordial Man (*El-Insânul-qadîm*), and just as Abraham is associated with Saturn, Adam is associated with the moon.[12] For the Chinese, the moon holds

---

[10] Betty War Brusa, *Salinan Indians of California and their Neighbors*, Happy Camp: Naturegraph, 2011, page 49. Of course, despite the presence of the padres, the return of this bird would amount to a fifth appearance.

[11] The largest flying land birds of North America are now restricted to California. We have already noted the giant redwood trees, formerly found in many lands, that found refuge in California. Similarly, the giant "California" condor once flew over all of North America, a remnant from a time when the animals it fed upon were larger, and the condor has sometimes been conflated with the Thunderbird. By the time it was "discovered" by American scientists, its range was restricted like the redwood, and was very nearly brought to extinction through the violence and poisonous ammunition of firearms and the chemical products of American science. Still, the bird is now experiencing a recovery thanks to human intervention, and the Yurok tribe in particular has been preparing to reintroduce it among the redwoods.

[12] Since the birds of the sun in the Chinese legend of Fusang are literally "sun crows" (and strangely three-footed), it is worth noting that according to Islamic lore, Adam introduces archery on earth by shooting at the crows plaguing his crops. It should also be noted that the meaning of the name "Adam" relates to red.

the secret to immortality, and the True Men are those who have regained the primordial state. It may be, then, that among its other more contingent meanings, what is indicated by the designation "Moon-eyed" is a capacity that John Michell called the "primordial vision" and that is inseparable from the Primordial Tradition:

> Thus are united the two sides of that whole which is symbolized by the Grail. With the primordial vision goes the primordial tradition. The first without the second provides a fleeting sensation of no lasting benefit; the second on its own is lifeless and without purpose. Together they may bring about the state of mind and perception which is appropriate to a golden age.[13]

Beginning with Columbus himself, the European arrivals in America could not ignore the nagging sense that the newly discovered lands promised nothing less than a lost Paradise. Sometimes this sense was accompanied by a vision of the "noble Indian" as most nearly approximating an Edenic state. To this day, in Germany for example, there are Europeans who imitate Indian culture as a hobby, but which nevertheless betrays a desire to recapture the primordial state. Others, such as the naturalist John Muir, preferred to ignore the American Indian tradition in his quest for the primordial vision. "Much has been written about that experience," observes Michell, "and many who have once known it have devoted lifetimes to regaining it, by methods ranging from asceticism to debauchery."[14] Yet it must be insisted that esoterism promises the permanent restoration of

---

[13] Michell and Rhone, page 10.
[14] Ibid., page 9. This last comment brings to mind a persistent modern error, namely the reliance upon the "fleeting sensations" of psychoactive substances in disregard of the Abrahamic traditions.

this state, and that a religious tradition that has forgotten this may no longer be considered as living.

In spite of this fleeting vision of America, the white man who seemed to be Bahana arrived on its shores without the piece of the Hopi tablet, a tablet that may be understood as an emblem of the Primordial Tradition.[15] After all, this tablet was said to be whole immediately following the Flood, recalling the singular source of the Hyperborean current; and despite the myriad traditional forms that subsequently arose, these all to a greater or lesser degree partake of the *din al-hanifi*. Put another way, the Christians had lost the Grail, that is, the emblem of Christianity's link to the Primordial Tradition and that is inseparable from Jesus, one of the ever-living Awtad. The treasure of the Templars is missing, and it is not without reason that it is still sought in the landscape of America.

In the greatest of the Grail legends, the *Parzival* by Wolfram von Eschenbach, the Grail is a stone from the sky, as we have already mentioned, and its power is explained very precisely in terms of the phoenix:

> By the power of that stone the phoenix burns to ashes, but the ashes give him life again. Thus does the phoenix molt and change its plumage, which afterward is bright and shining and lovely as before. There never was a human so ill but that, if he one day sees that stone, he cannot die within the week that follows…Such power does the stone give a man that flesh and bones are at once made young again.[16]

---

[15] It will be observed that the tablets of Joseph Smith, as well as other suspect discoveries in America, are but parodies of this reality.
[16] Translated by Mustard and Passage, New York: Vintage Books, 1961, pages 251-2. Of course, this description recalls the methods and goals of the Taoist alchemists.

The Western Phoenix

The rise of the Western Phoenix at the end of time announces a new Golden Age. Whereas the moon is an emblem of the primordial condition for the microcosm, for the world of the macrocosm its restoration is expressed in solar terms, and so by the Bahana wearing red. The Western Sun and the "Seal of Sainthood" who is none other than Jesus govern this alchemical reddening. Jesus returns with the power to slay with his spear[17] the Anti-Christ who misrepresents him; and although Jesus was without doubt a healer in his historical appearance, only with his apocalyptic return does he bring healing for the macrocosm, establishing a "Heavenly Kingdom on Earth."

How far removed from this healing was the historical invasion of America by Christians, and whose final movement West was a rush for a very different gold.[18] Still, how strangely promising that the name "California" was chosen for the land that is the last to be reached by the westering sun, since it derives from the Arabic title "caliph" that indicates not only the primordial condition of humanity, but more immediately the one who *"fills the earth with equality and justice, as it has been filled with injustice and oppression."*[19]

---

[17] This choice of weapon mentioned in the Traditions most nearly approximates the symbol of the *watad* ("stake").

[18] This parody invites another observation. It has been mentioned that the name of the Cherokee sacerdotal caste was "People of Kutánî", with "Kutánî" being an unknown word. However, the word does appear in Arabic, and its root extends not only to "Indian corn," but also to "cotton," and is in fact the source of the latter word. Now, it may be observed that the cotton industry became the foremost excuse for the institution of slavery in America, through which scores of Arabic speakers suffered. This institution brought evil both to its perpetrators and victims, Muslim and Christian, and so was inimical to the family of Abraham. For this reason, the domination of white "King Cotton" in the lands of the Cherokee seems to mock the memory of the People of Kutánî.

[19] Sahih Tradition.

www.ingramcontent.com/pod-product-compliance
Lightning Source LLC
LaVergne TN
LVHW021120080426
835510LV00012B/1772